D0100076

ARE YOU READY?
CRAYON

This Chronicle Books edition published in 2006.

Originally published in the United States in 2004 by Seuil/Chronicle under the
ISBN 2-02-061396-4.

Originally published in Japan in 1990 by Bronze Publishing Inc.
under the title *Rakugaki Ehon*.

Copyright © 1990 by Taro Gomi.
All rights reserved.

Translation by Shoshanna Kirk-Jegousse.
Typeset in Avenir.

Manufactured in Singapore.

ISBN-13 978-0-8118-5509-9
ISBN-10 0-8118-5509-0

10 9 8 7 6 5 4

Chronicle Books LLC
680 Second Street, San Francisco, California 94107

www.chroniclekids.com

Scribbles

A Really Giant Drawing and Coloring Book

chronicle books · san francisco

This is a tree

Fill it with leaves

This man needs a moustache

This one needs hair

Draw some zigzags

Color these hats

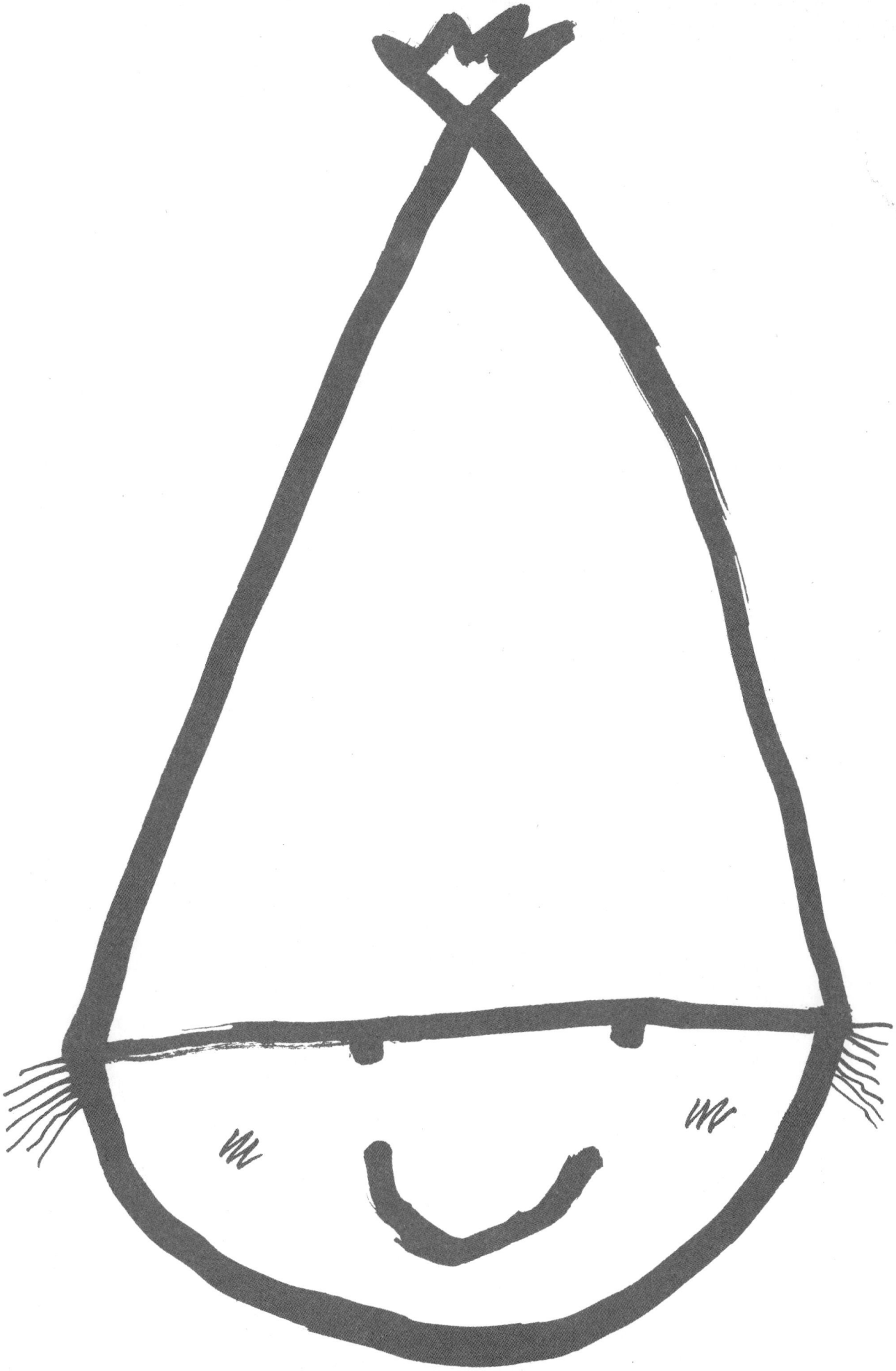

These children need clothes

These people do, too

Can you draw them a bridge?

Draw some flowers

Draw butterflies, too

Draw big summer clouds

Draw the road

Color the circles

And try to stay within the lines

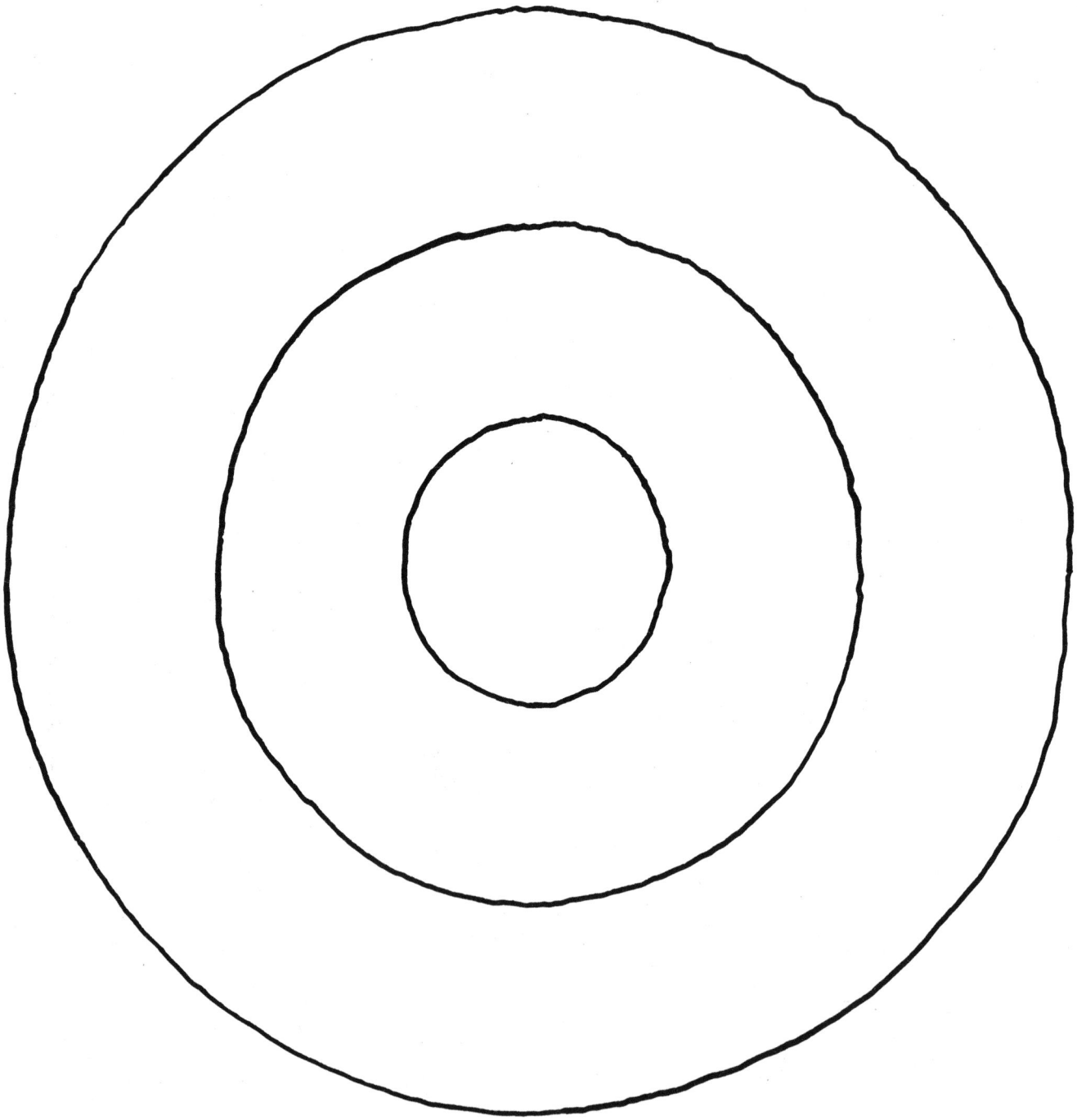

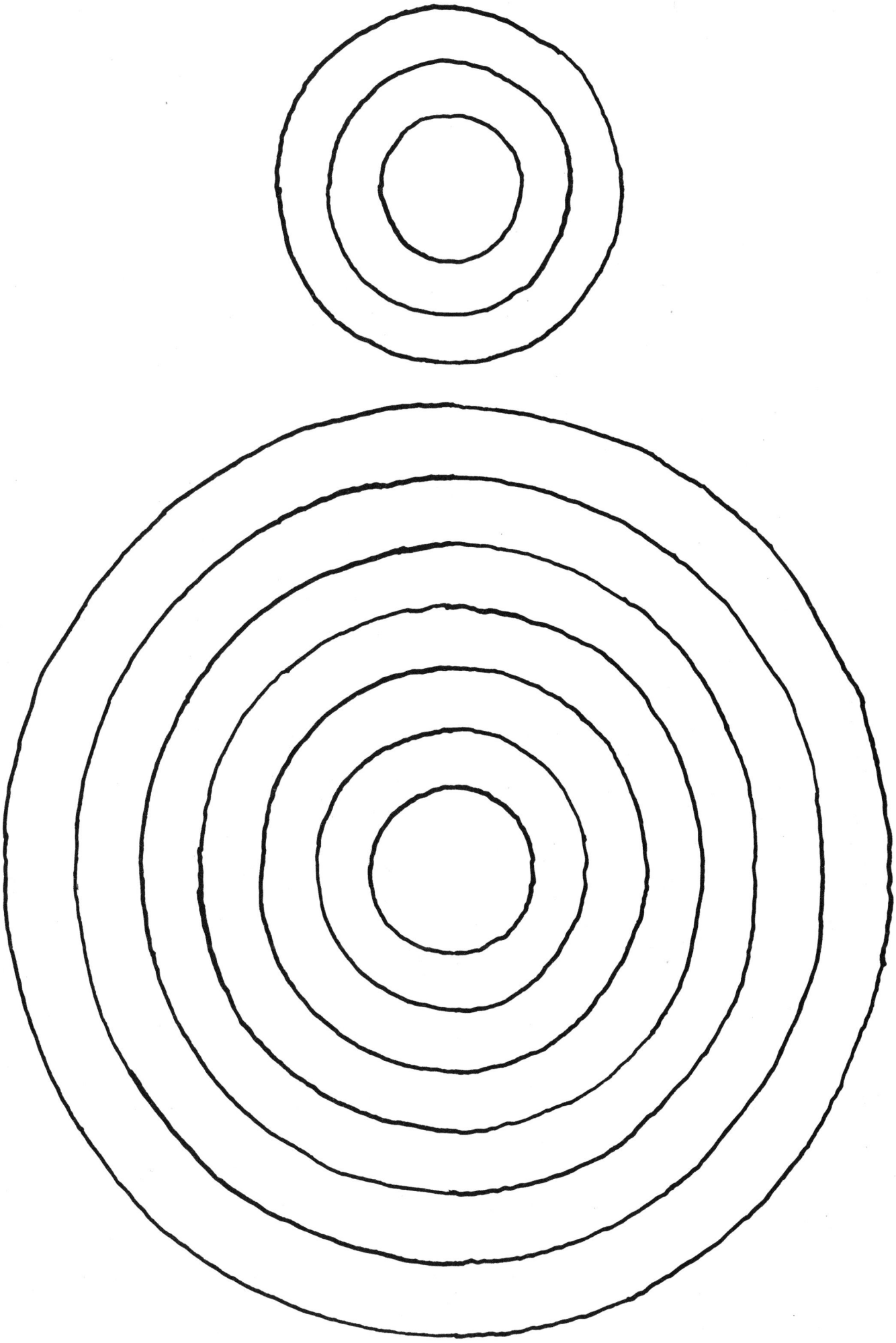

Who is looking out the windows?

It's three o'clock

Draw the hands on the clock

Now, it's eight-thirty

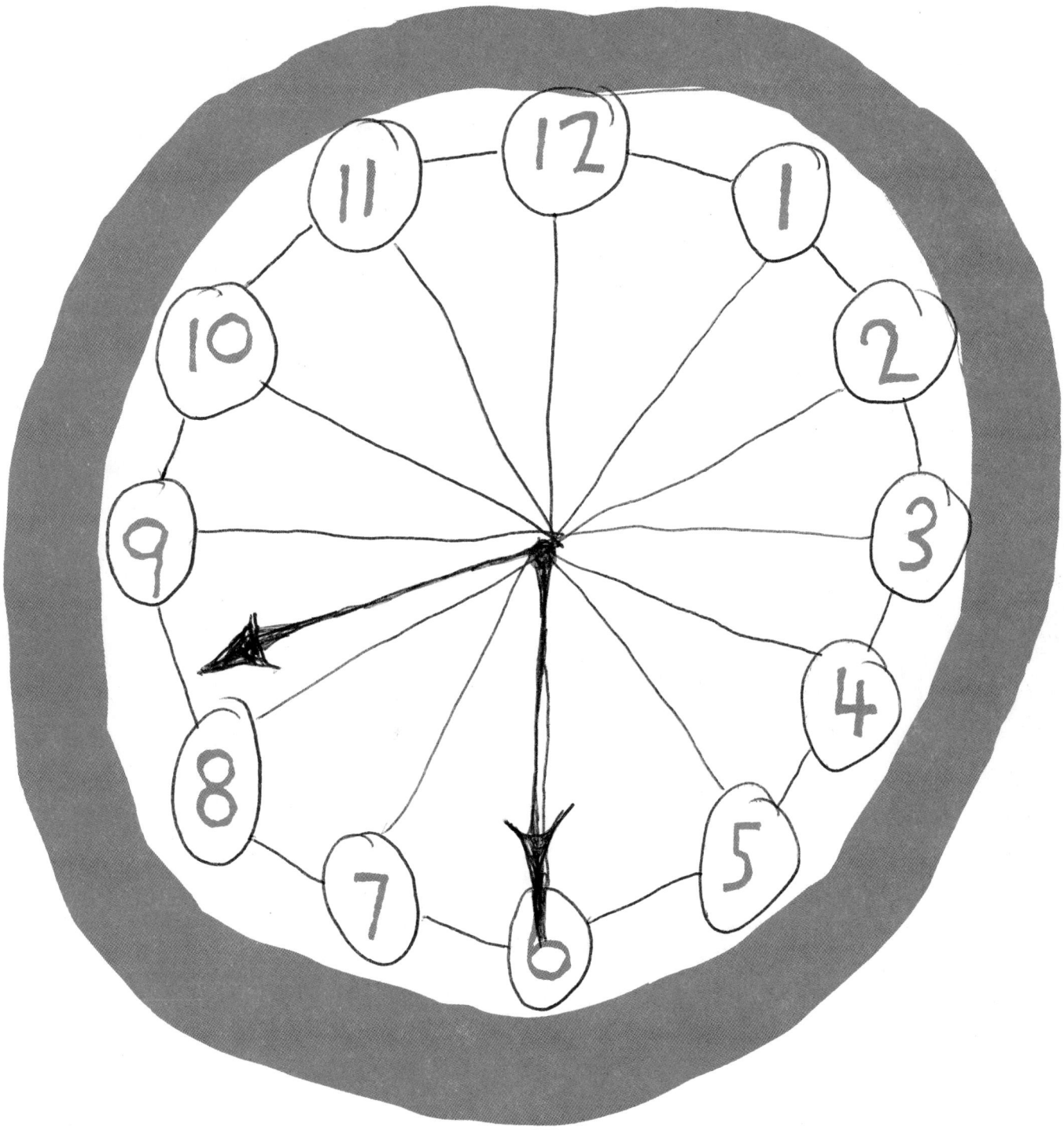

Color this using pastel colors

Draw something good to eat

It's raining

Draw the rain pouring down

These are robots

They need arms and legs

I need a hat

Draw him a hat

I need a ribbon

Draw her a ribbon

Draw bubbles

Draw a balloon

Draw some teeth

Draw some cavities (on the teeth!)

It's a beautiful day today

Draw a bright sunny sky

Today, it's not so nice

Draw a dark cloudy sky

Today, there's a thunderstorm

Draw lightening and rain

This is the sea

Draw some boats

Oh no! It's a wolf!

Make sure he doesn't eat the pigs!

Use this triangle to draw something

Now, use this square

It's snowing!

Draw a snake

Make it longer than this piece of rope

Draw an insect

Make it smaller than this little stone

Draw a dragonfly sitting on top of this pole

Draw a crocodile balancing on top of this pole

Draw a huge volcanic eruption

Copy this!

Draw exactly the same thing on the right-hand page

Draw people sitting down

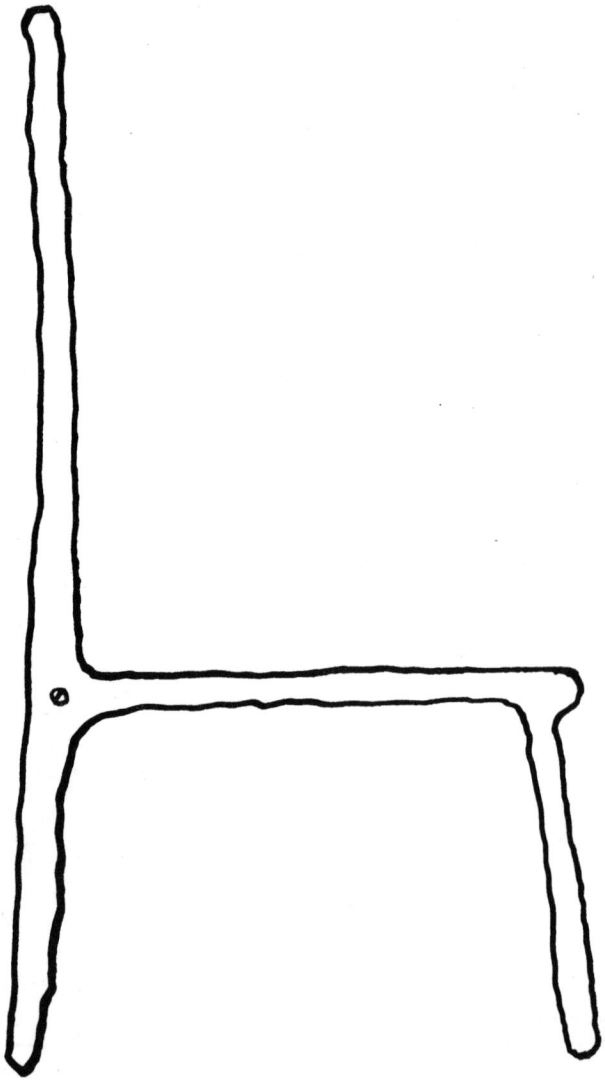

Fill this tree with birds

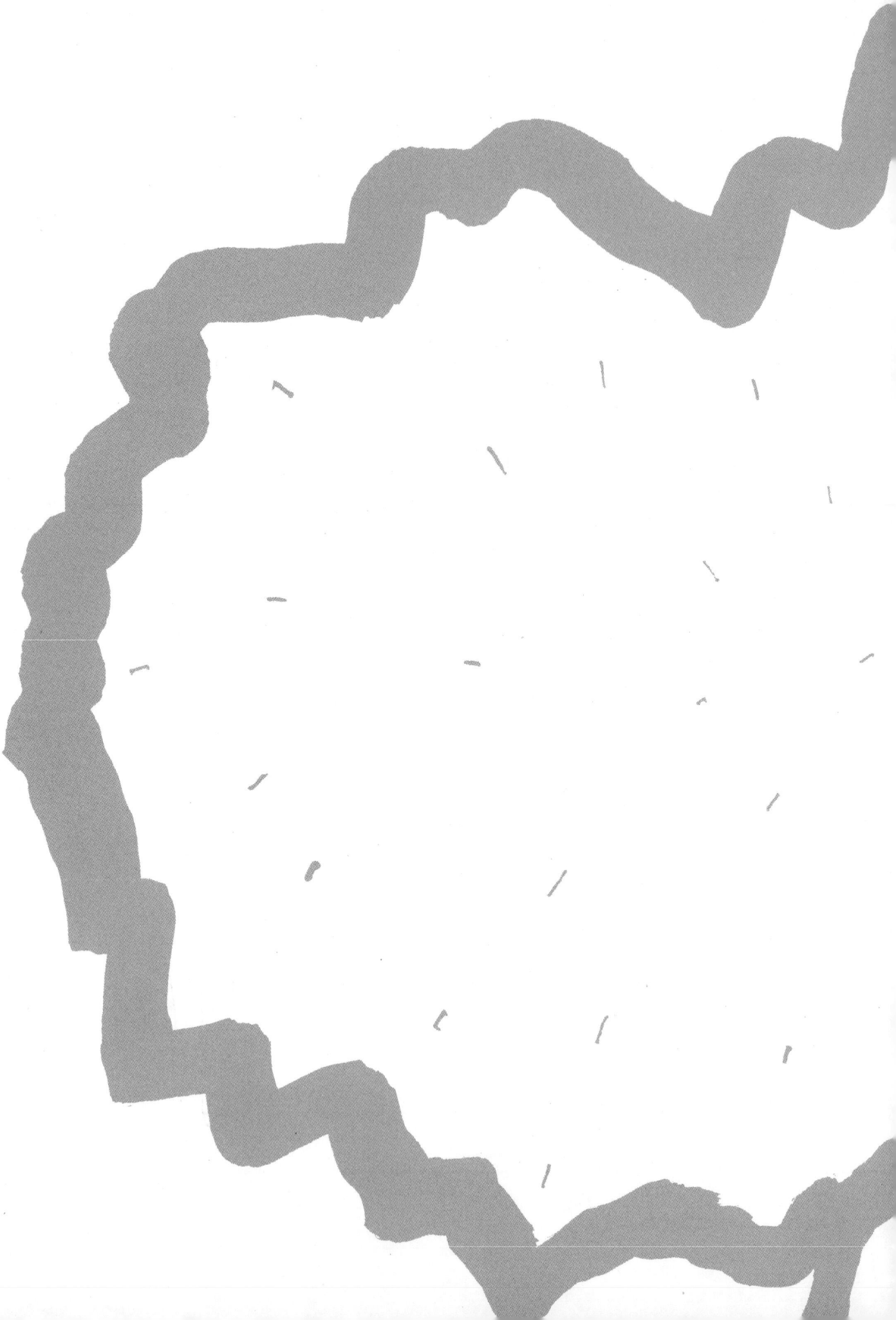

Draw houses in this landscape

Draw fields, schools and buildings, too

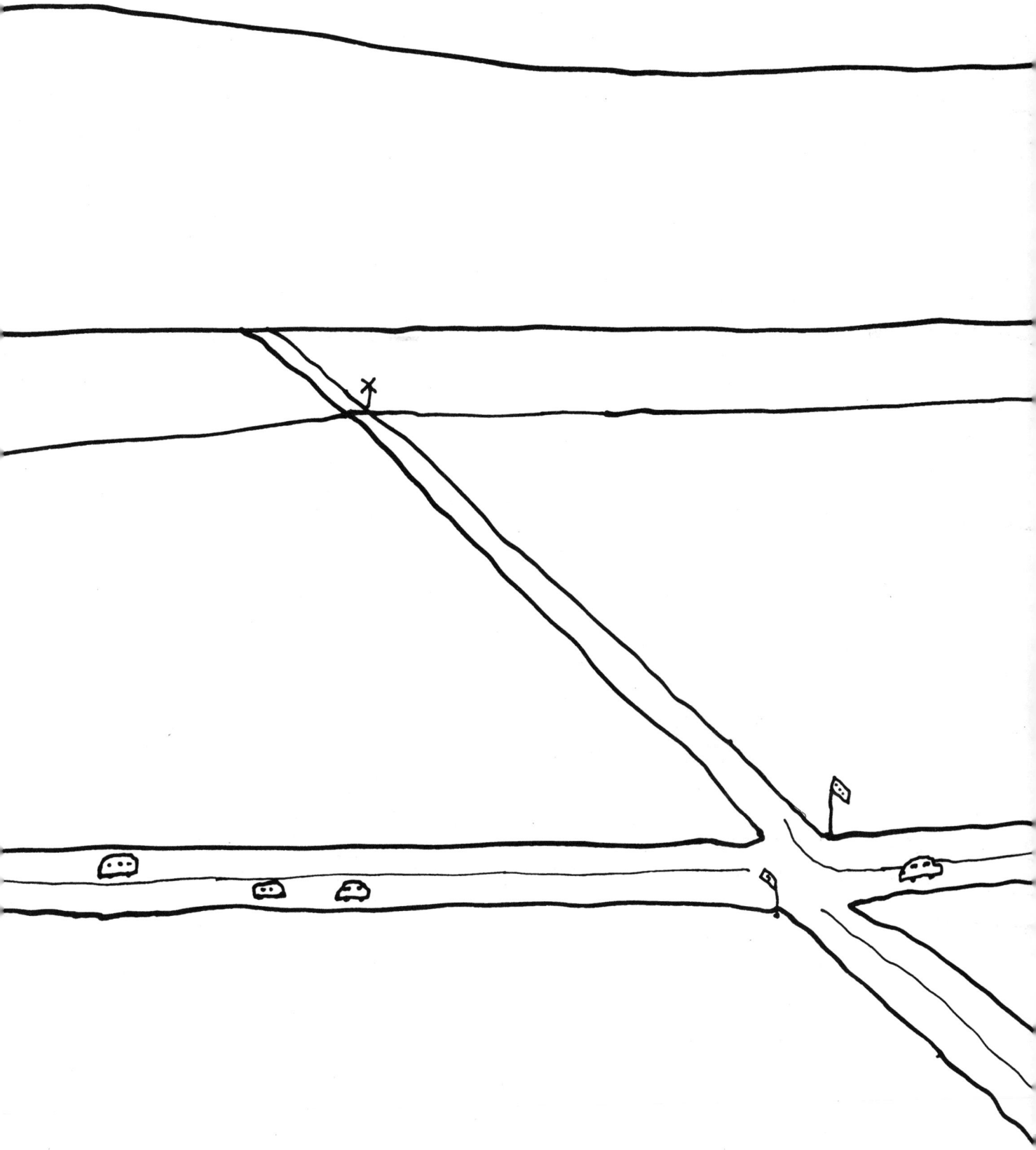

This is a mountain

Cover it with trees

This is a staircase

Draw people walking up

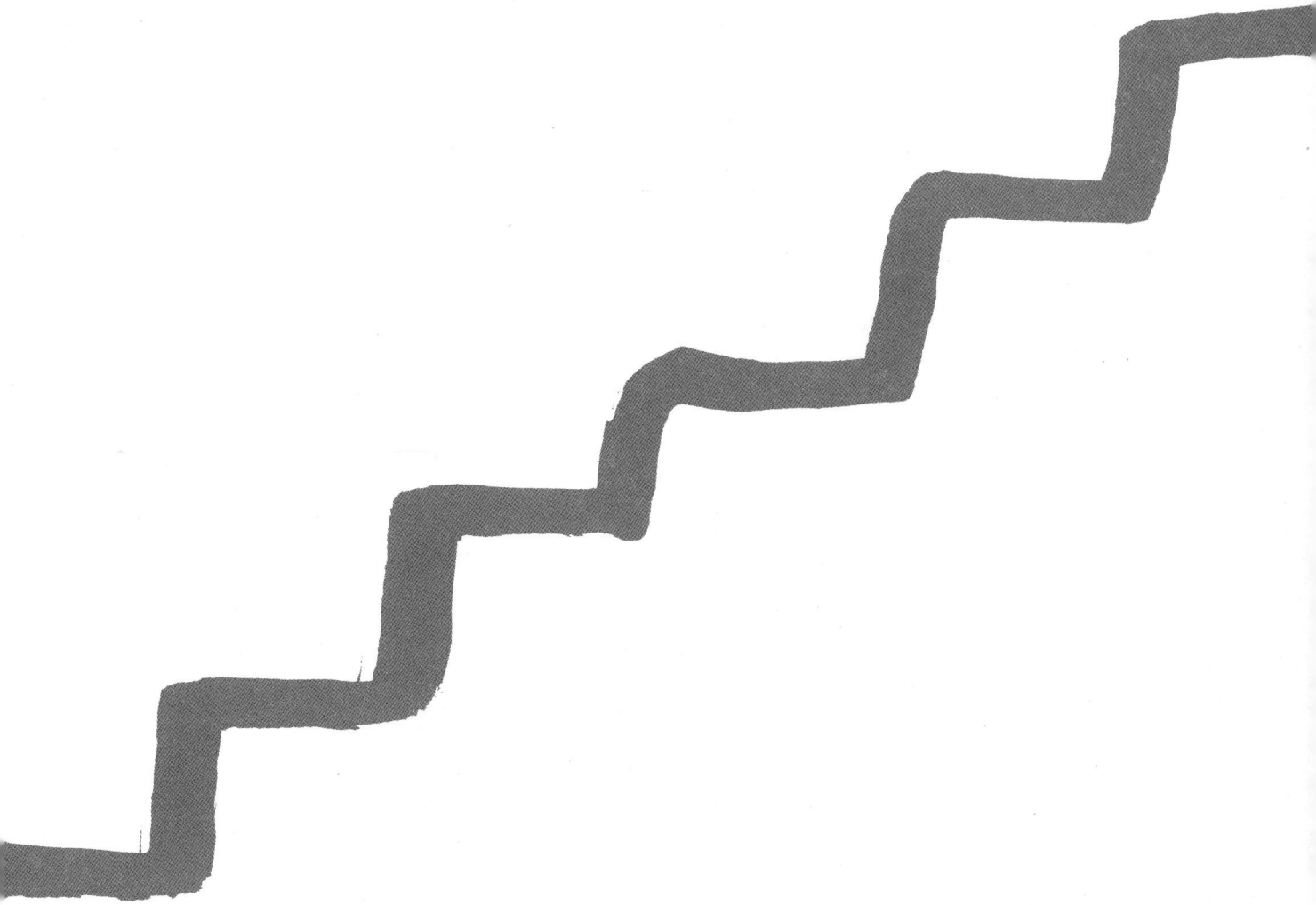

This is a staircase, too

Draw people walking down, and some people falling!

Draw a rainbow

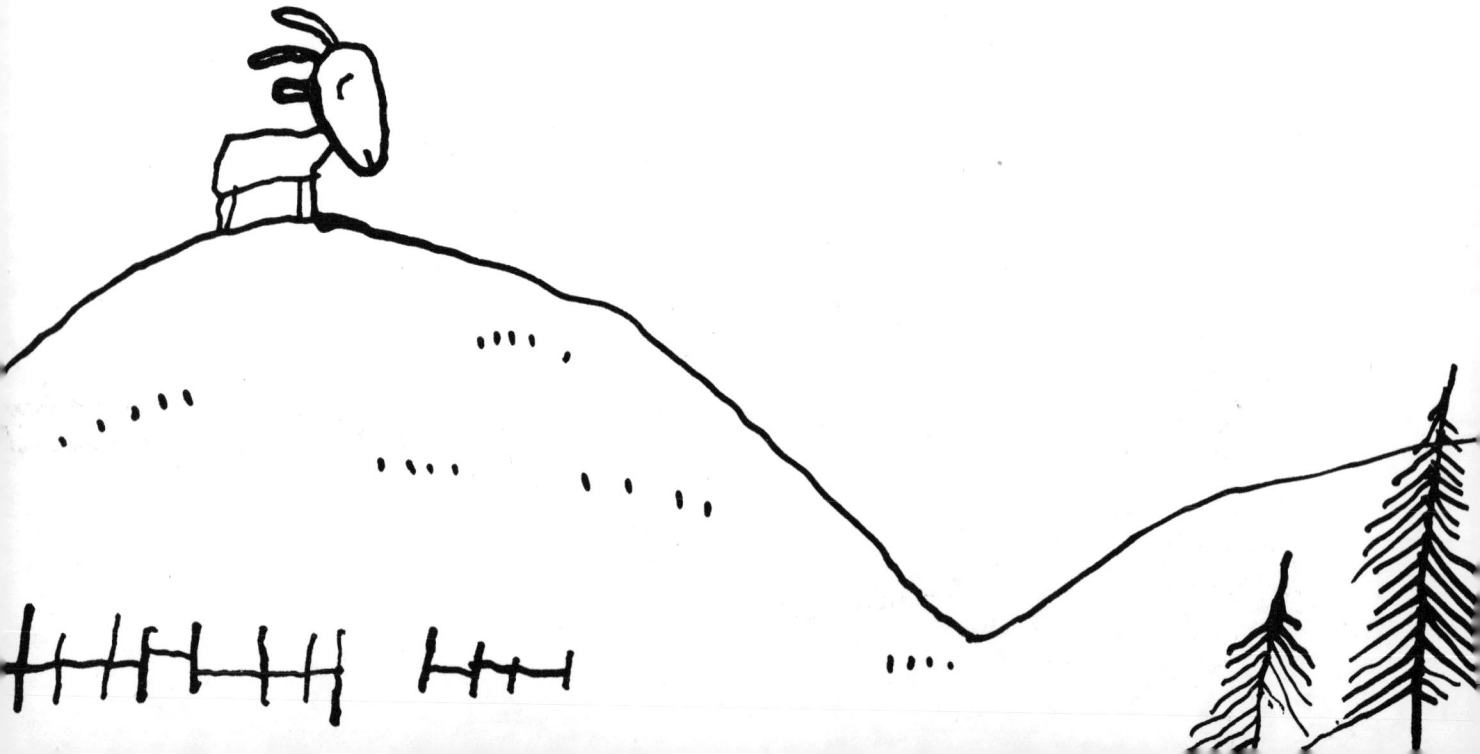

I am an octopus

Draw my tentacles

I am a squid

I need tentacles, too

Draw an airplane

Color these crayons

With crayons!

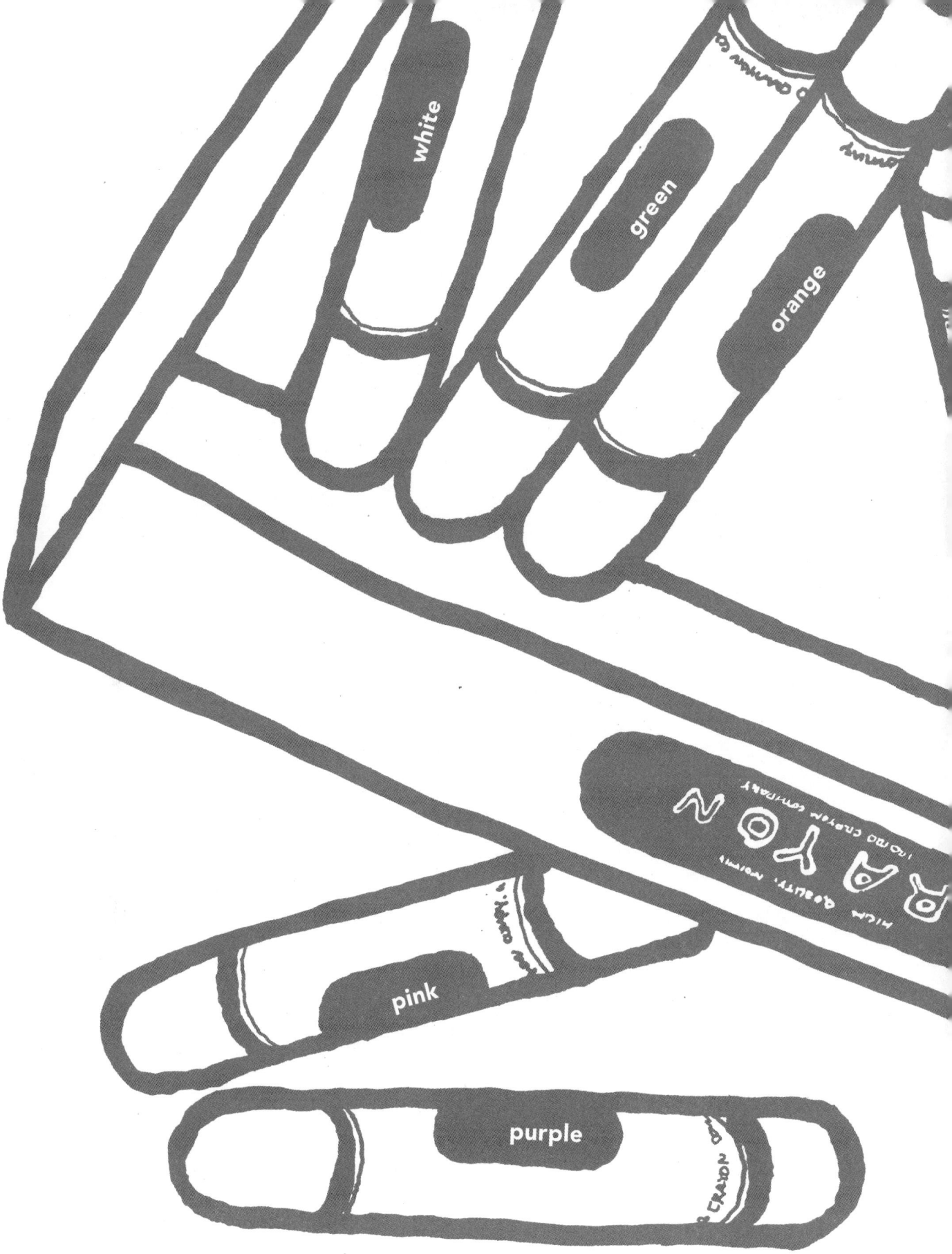
white
green
orange
pink
purple

I'm five years old

Put five candles on my cake

HAPPY
BIRTHDAY

Color these vegetables

This is a color game

Follow this code

★ red ● yellow ■ blue
▲ green ◉ orange ▣ purple

Don't use the wrong color!

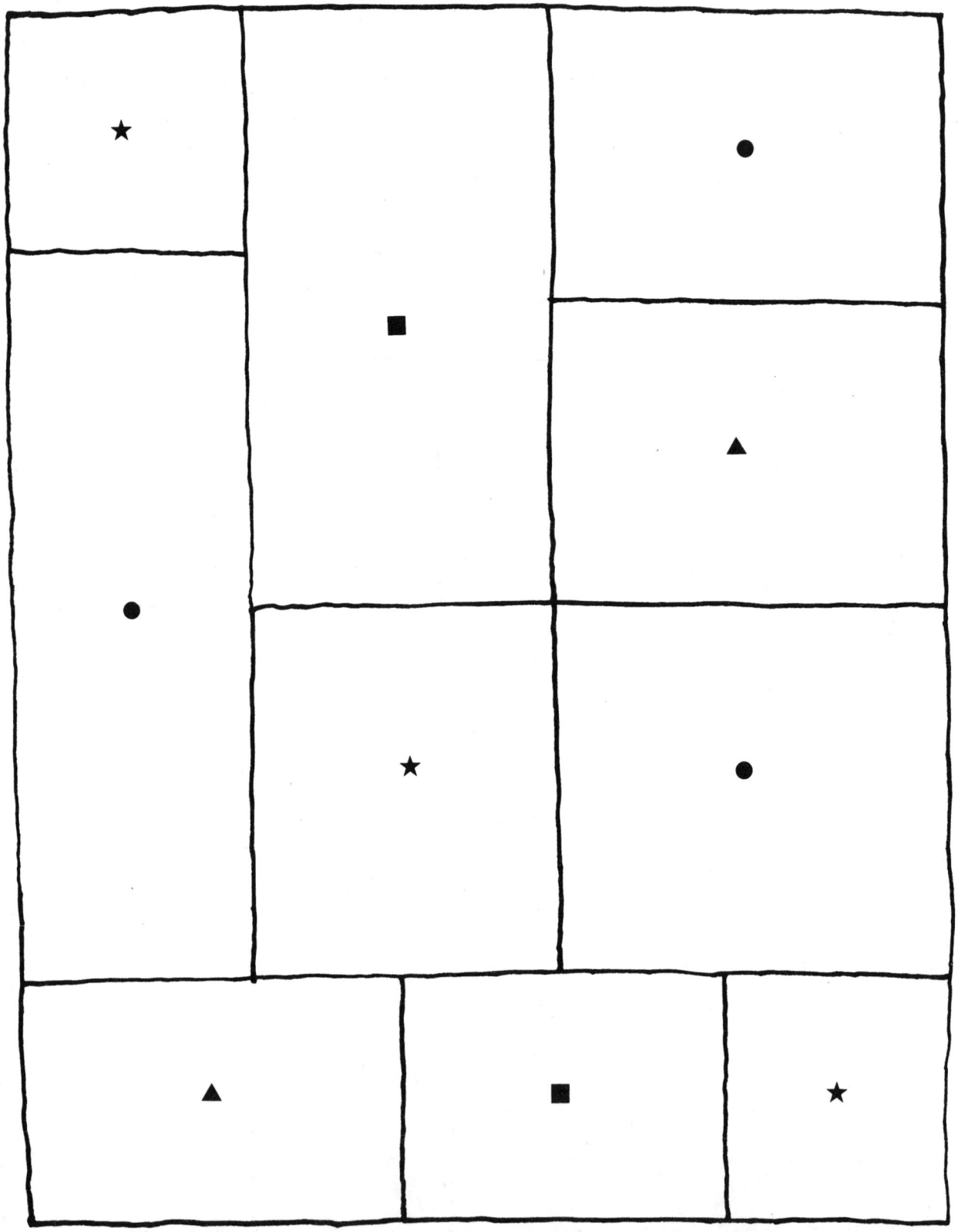

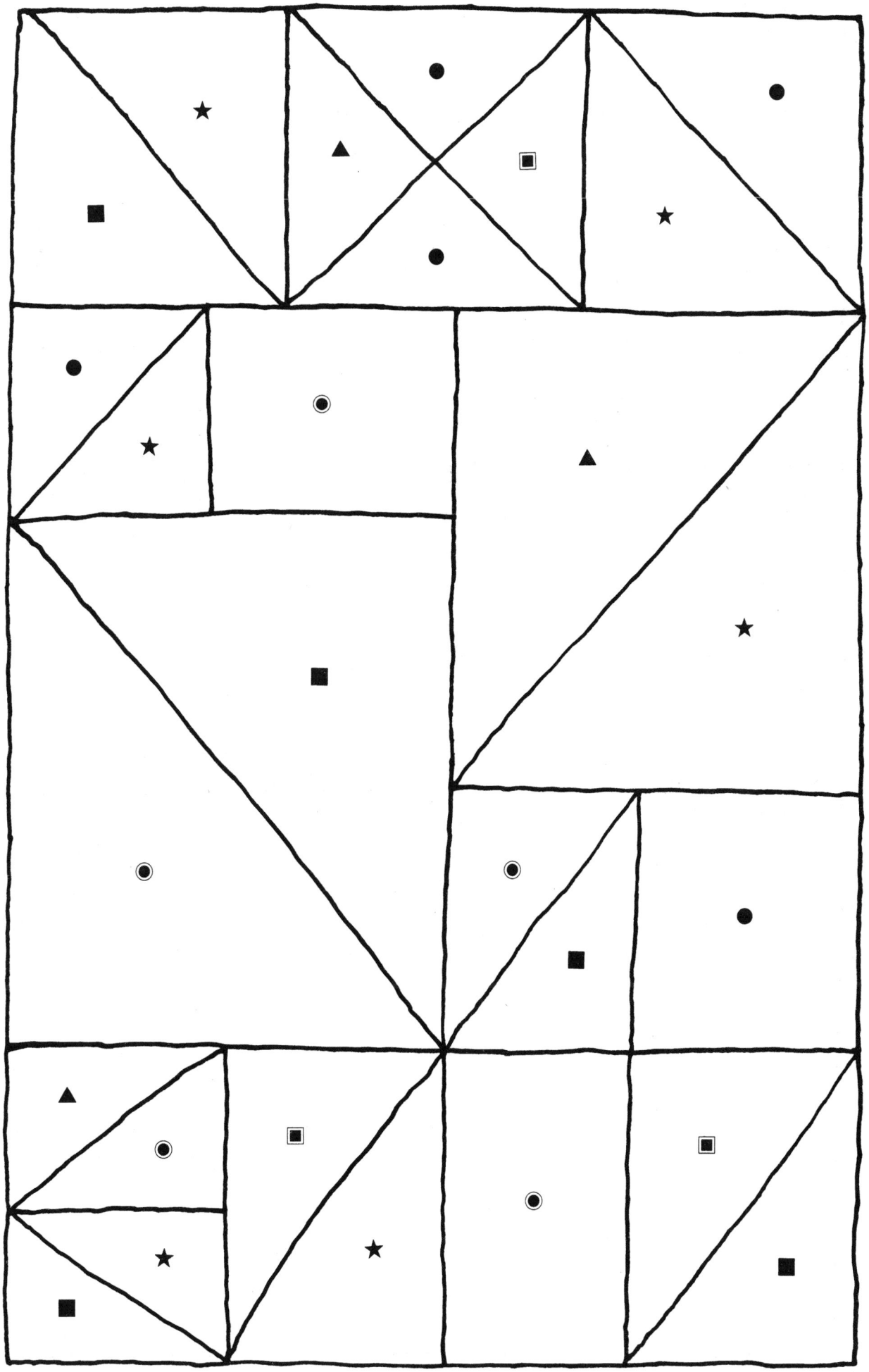

Draw some windows

Paint the walls

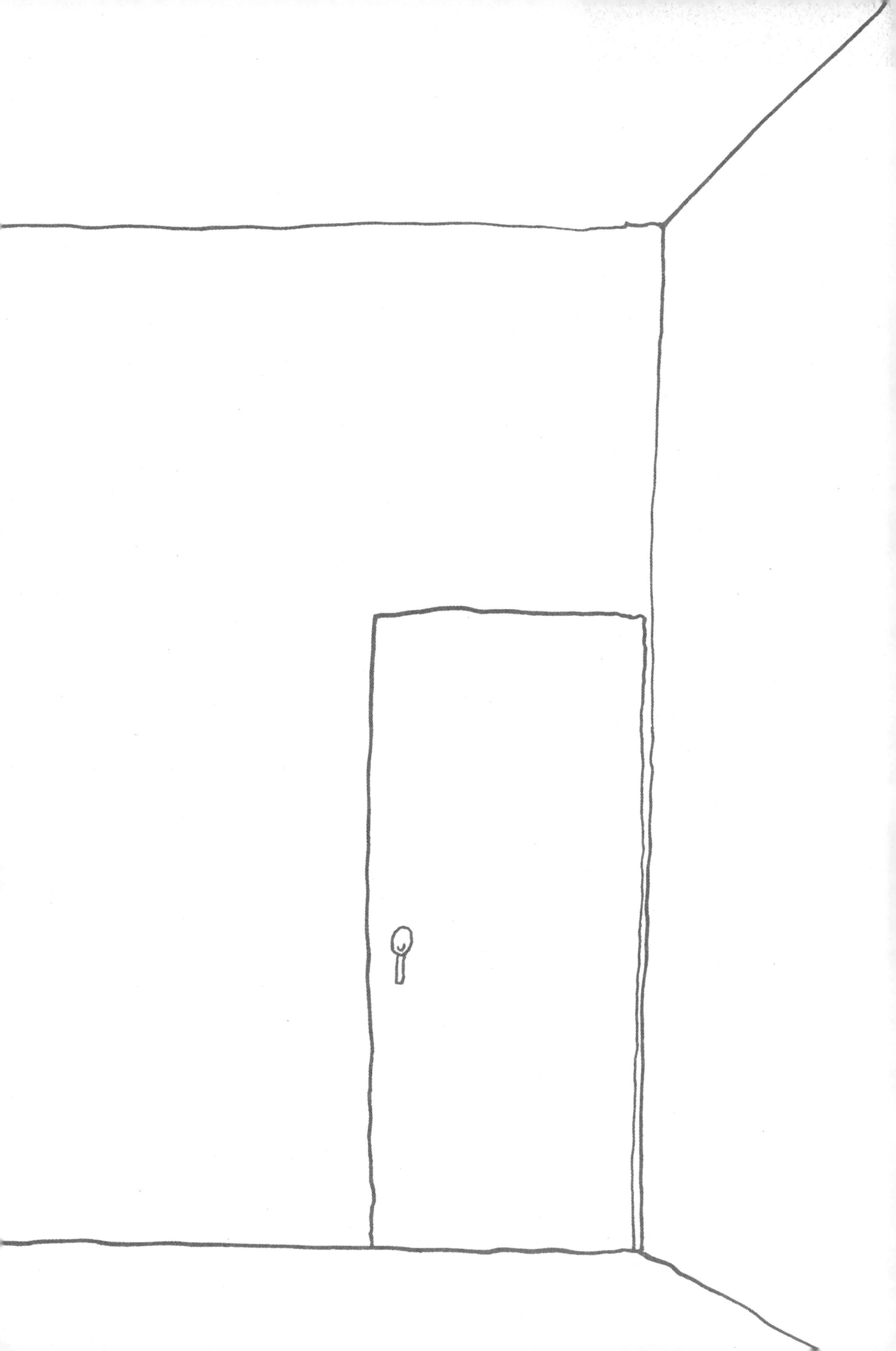

Draw some cars

This horse needs legs

And a tail!

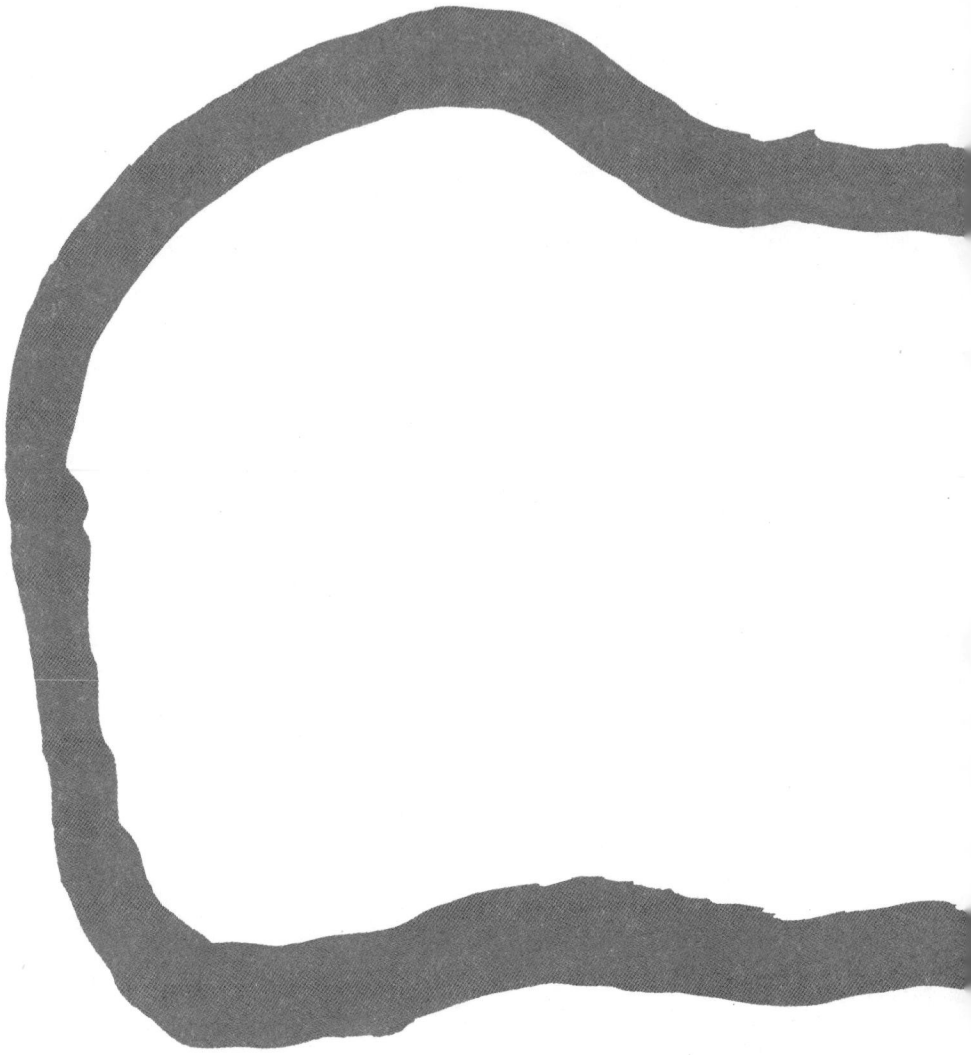

Draw something curly

Draw something that spirals

Draw an angry face

Draw a sad face

Color only the things you like

えほん
WHISKY
9744

Draw some monsters

Draw an invisible man

Color with bright colors

Color with pale colors

Draw a bright sun

Make some rockets fly

Draw some flags

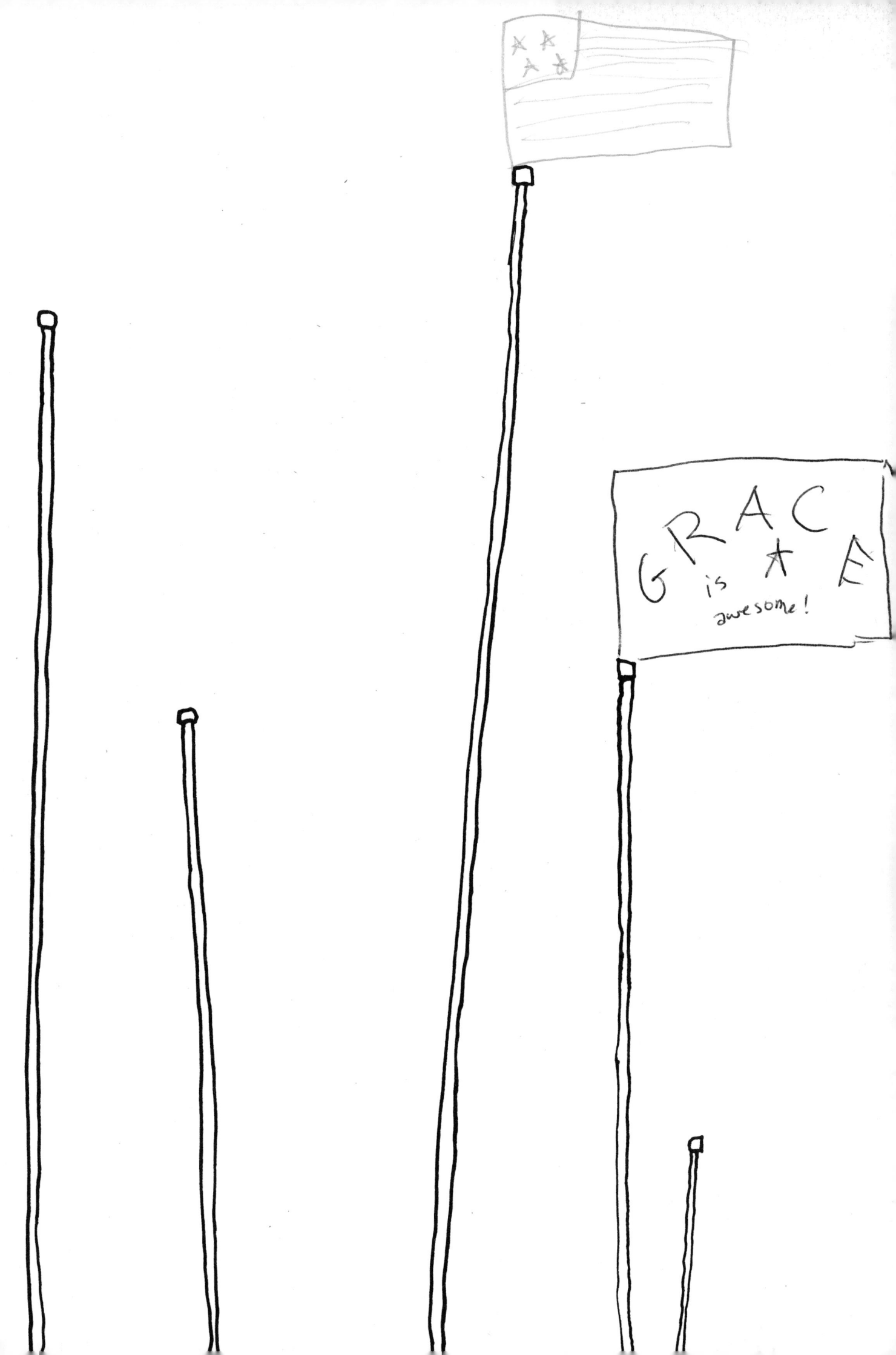
GRACE
is
awesome!

Draw their faces

Make the woman as friendly and the man as scary as you can

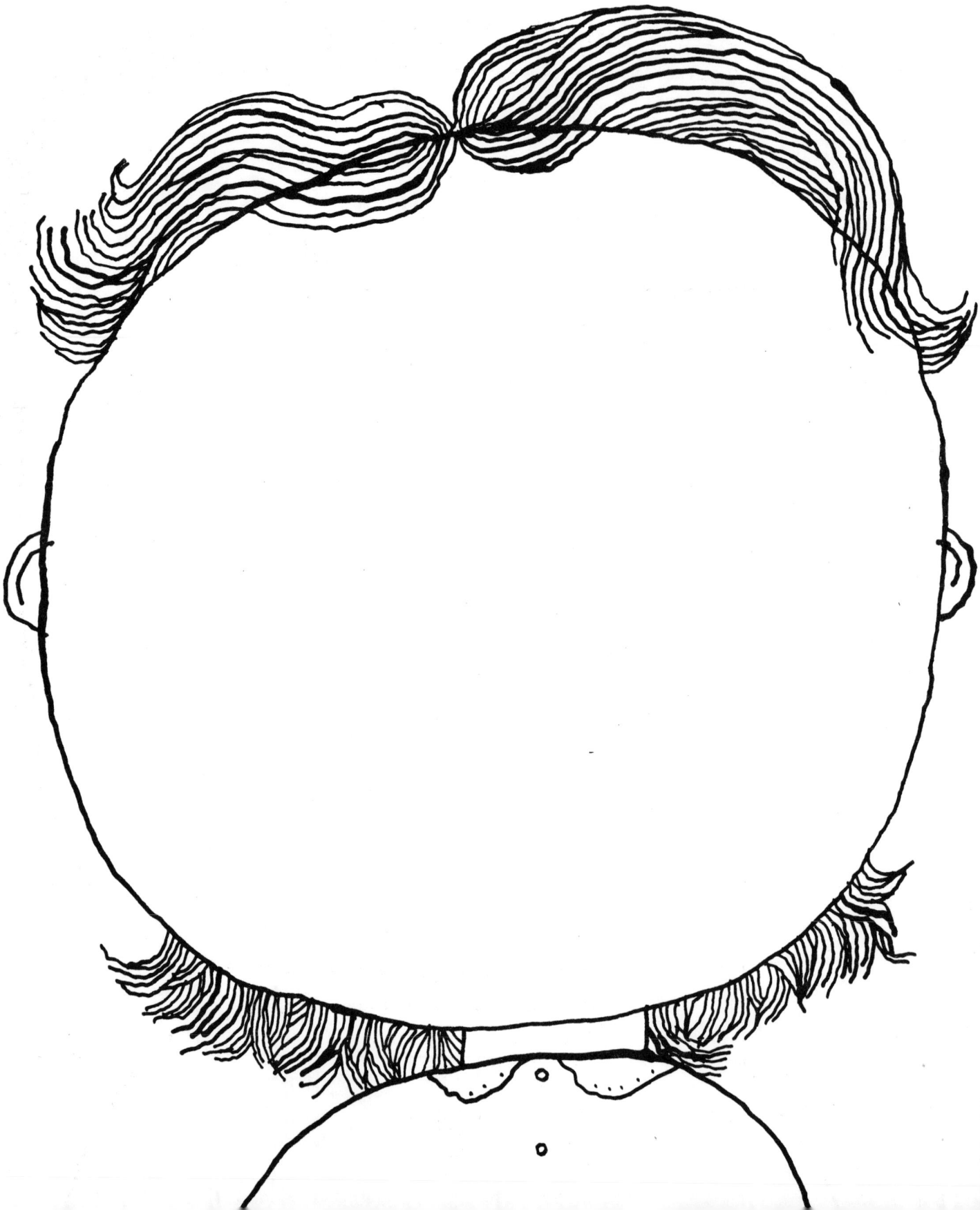

Draw patterns on their clothes

LEGO

Draw some things that are round

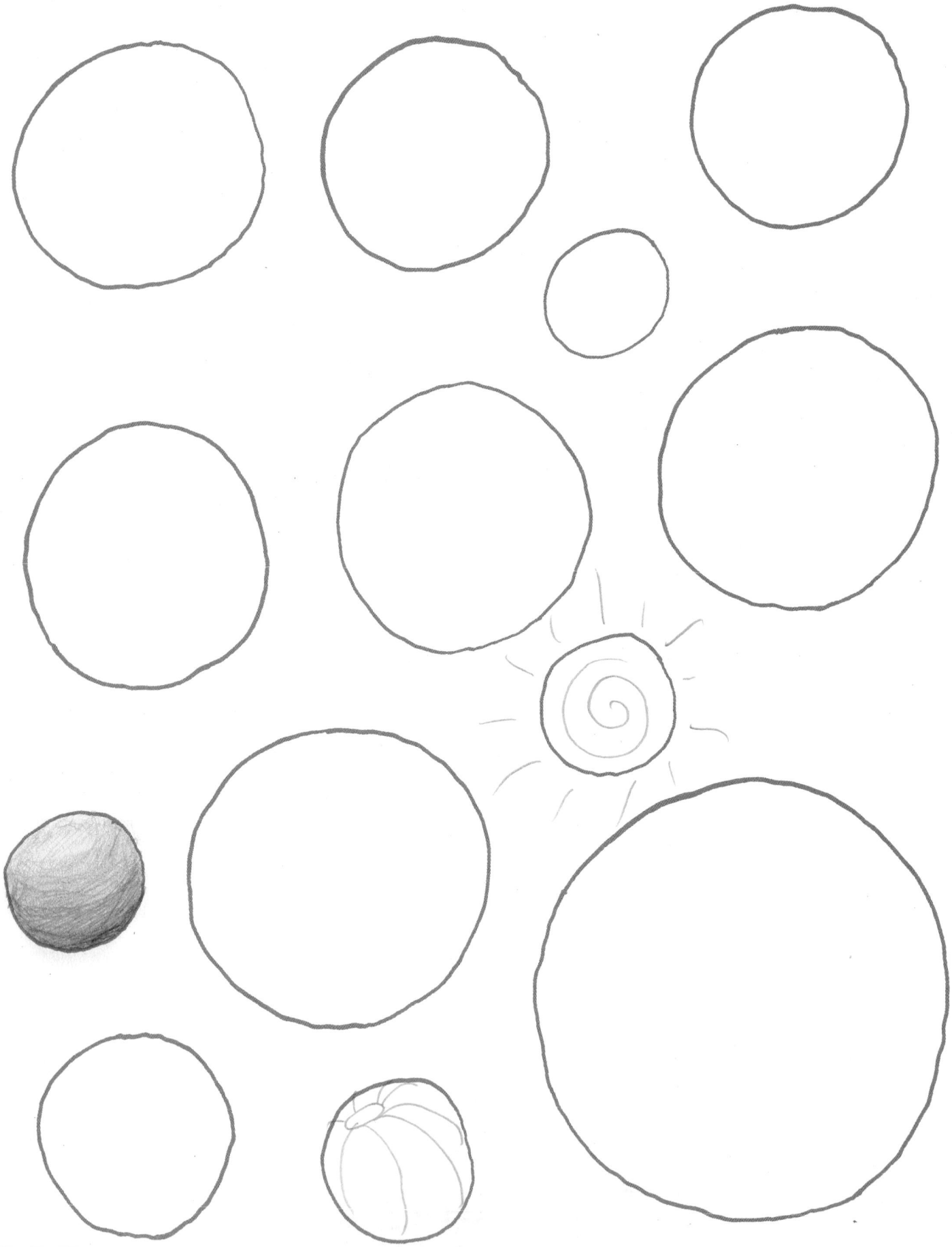

12
1
2
3
4
5
6
7
8
9
10
11

Draw sails on these boats

poseidon?

Draw tufts of grass

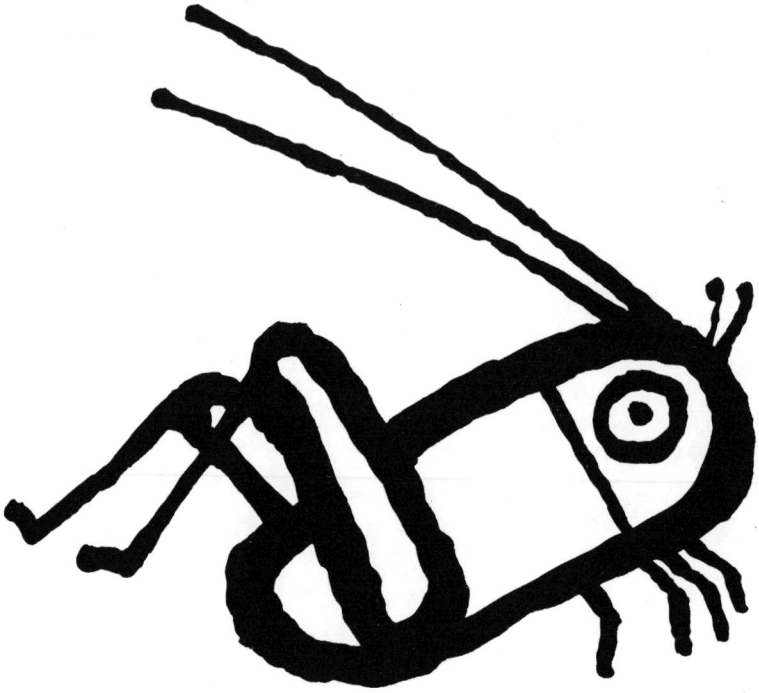

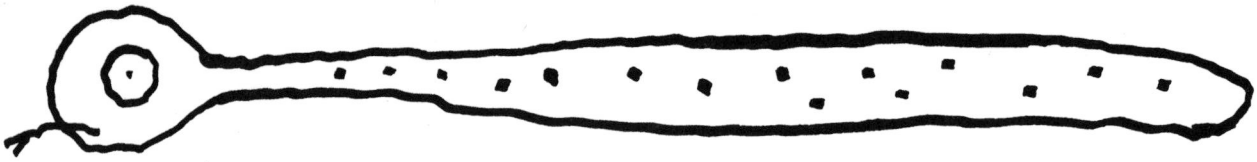

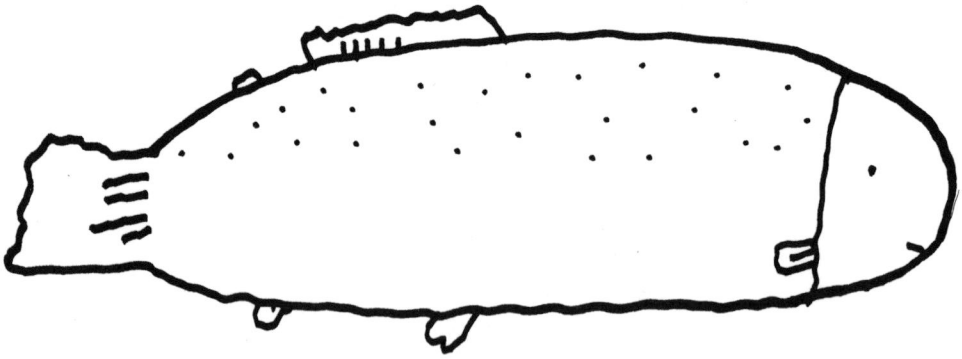

Draw feathers and a tail on this boy

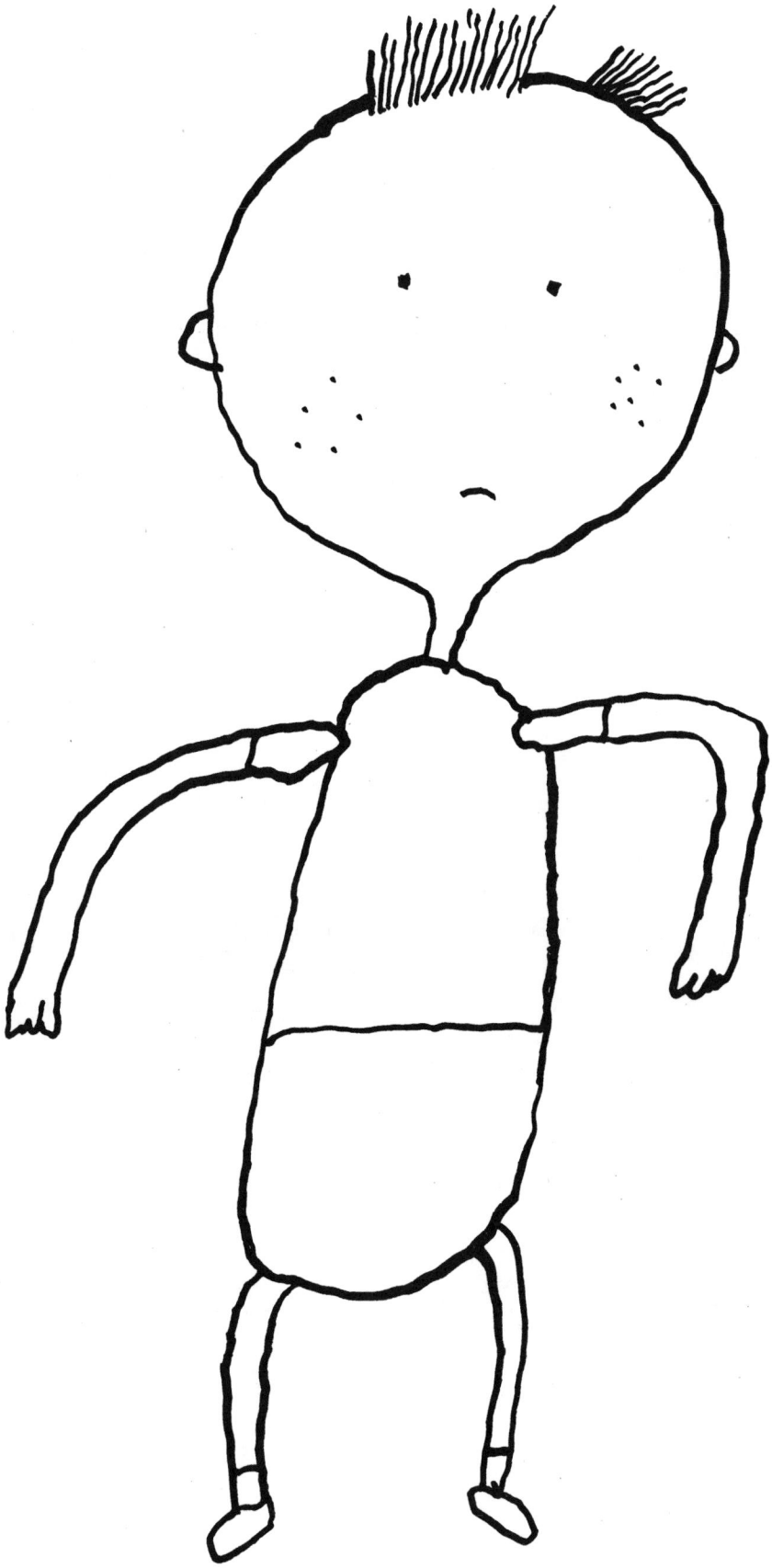

Draw the passengers on the bus

Fill the picnic basket

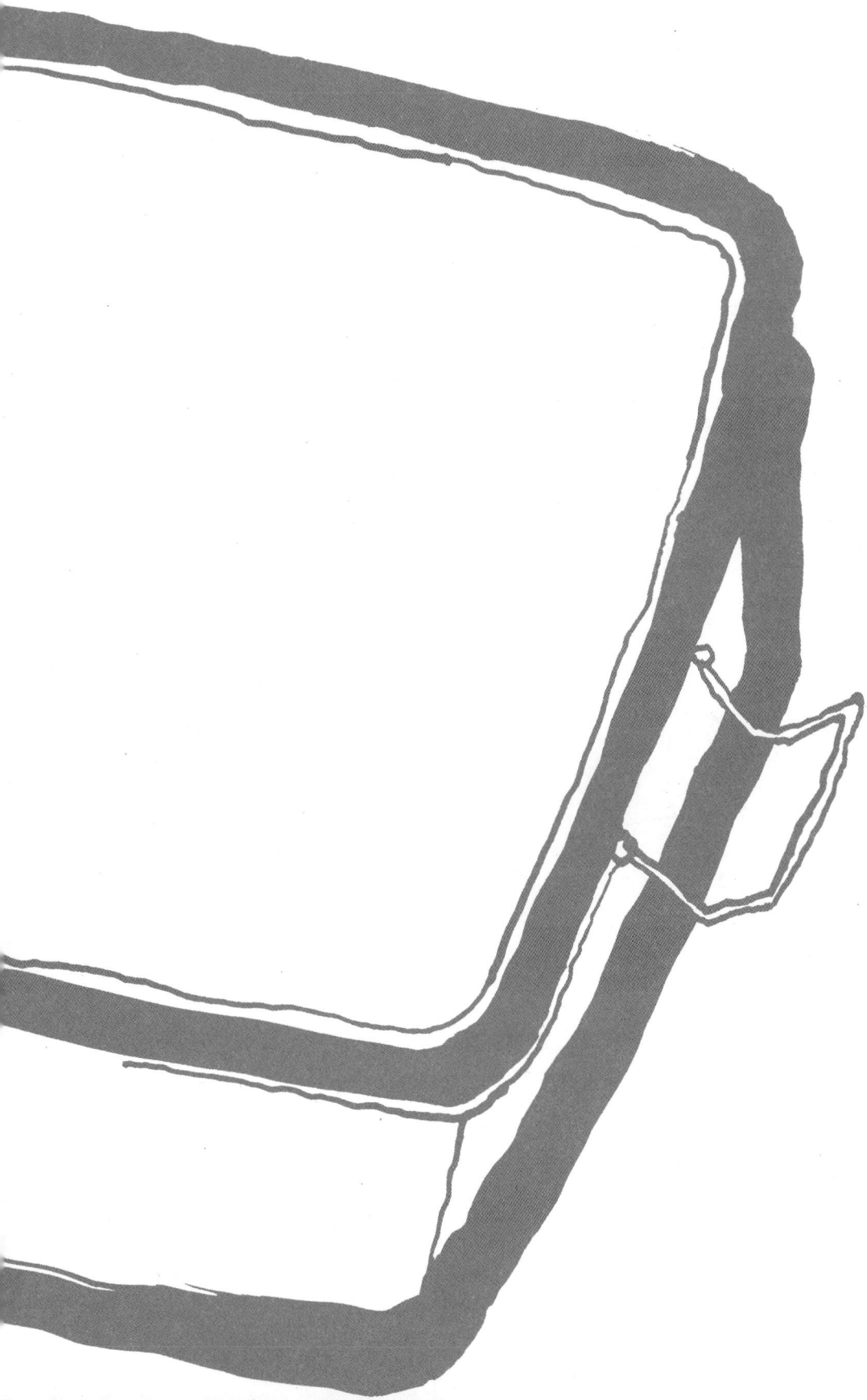

Draw lines going every which way

The moon has risen

Draw some people walking down the road

And some tired people resting along the way

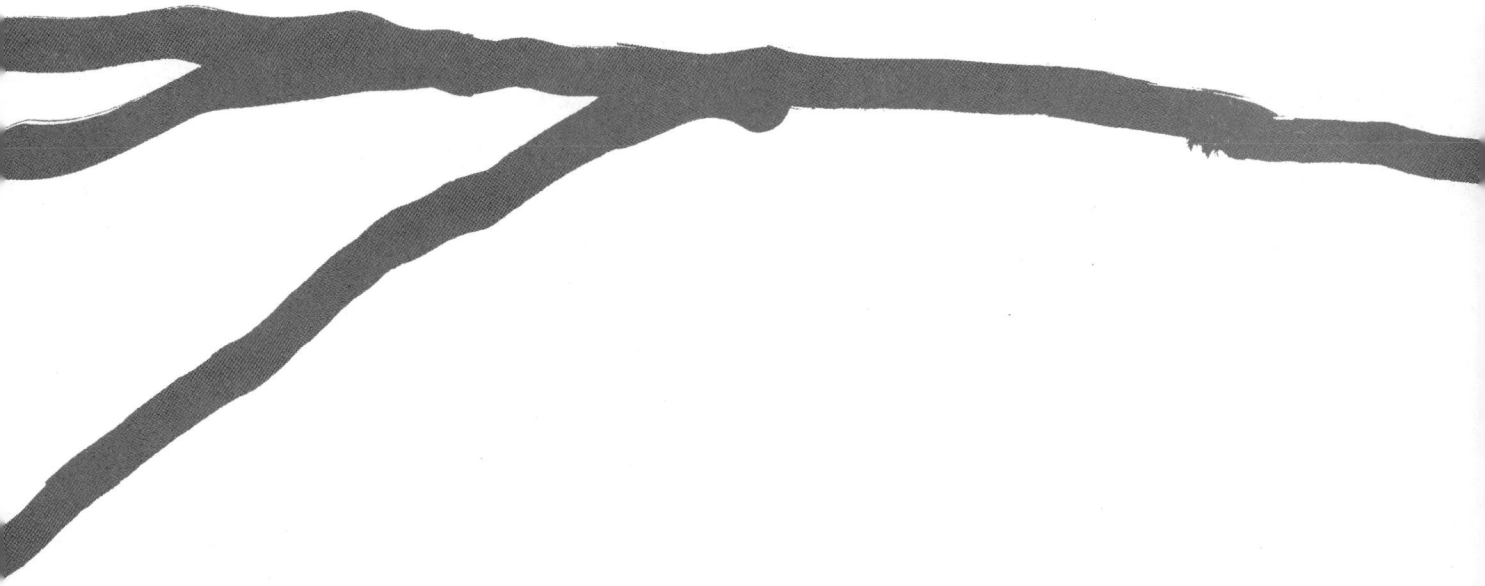

Make the lion look strong

Make up a recipe using rice

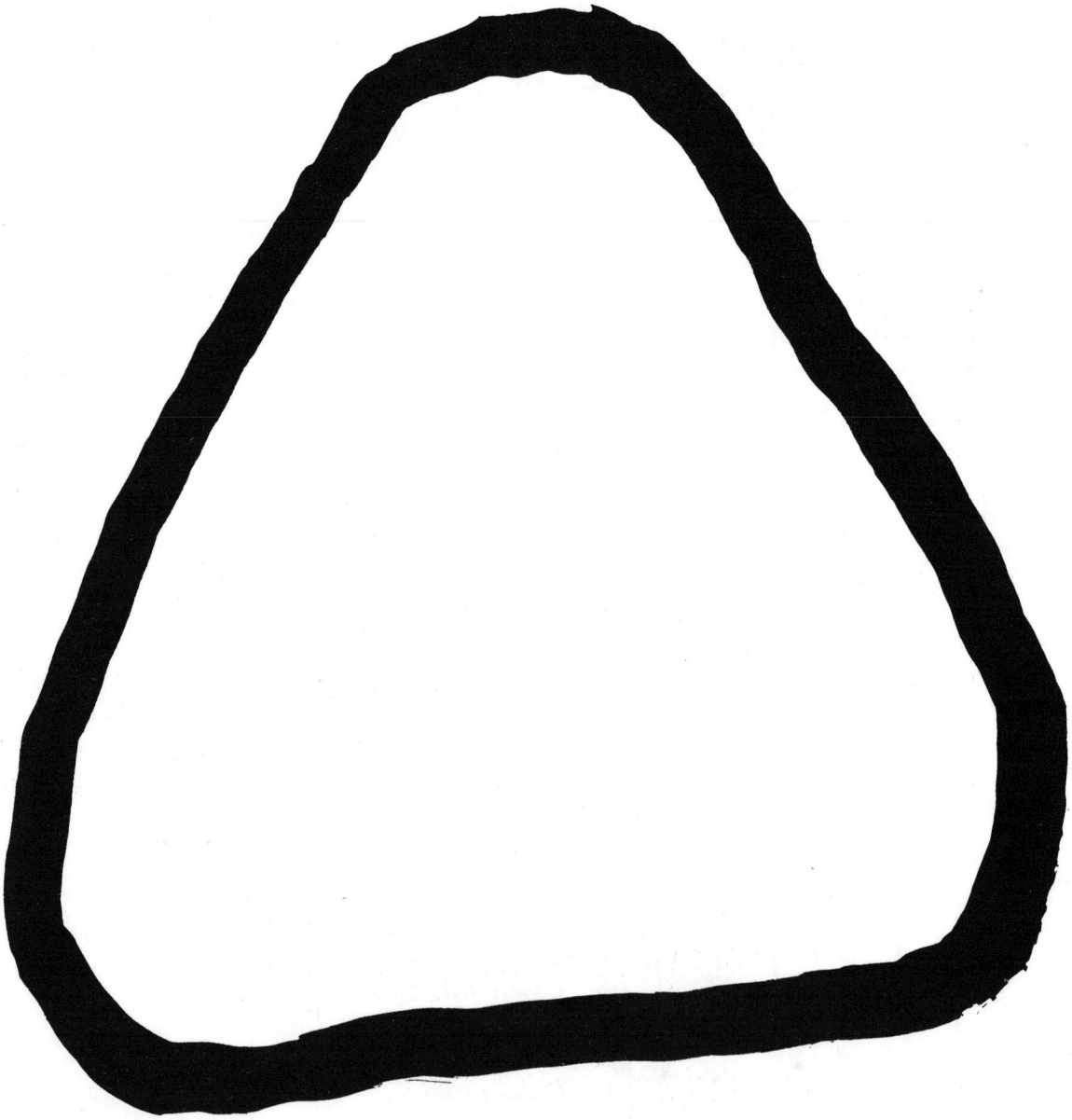

Draw the finished dish

Ouch! That hurt!

Draw bandages

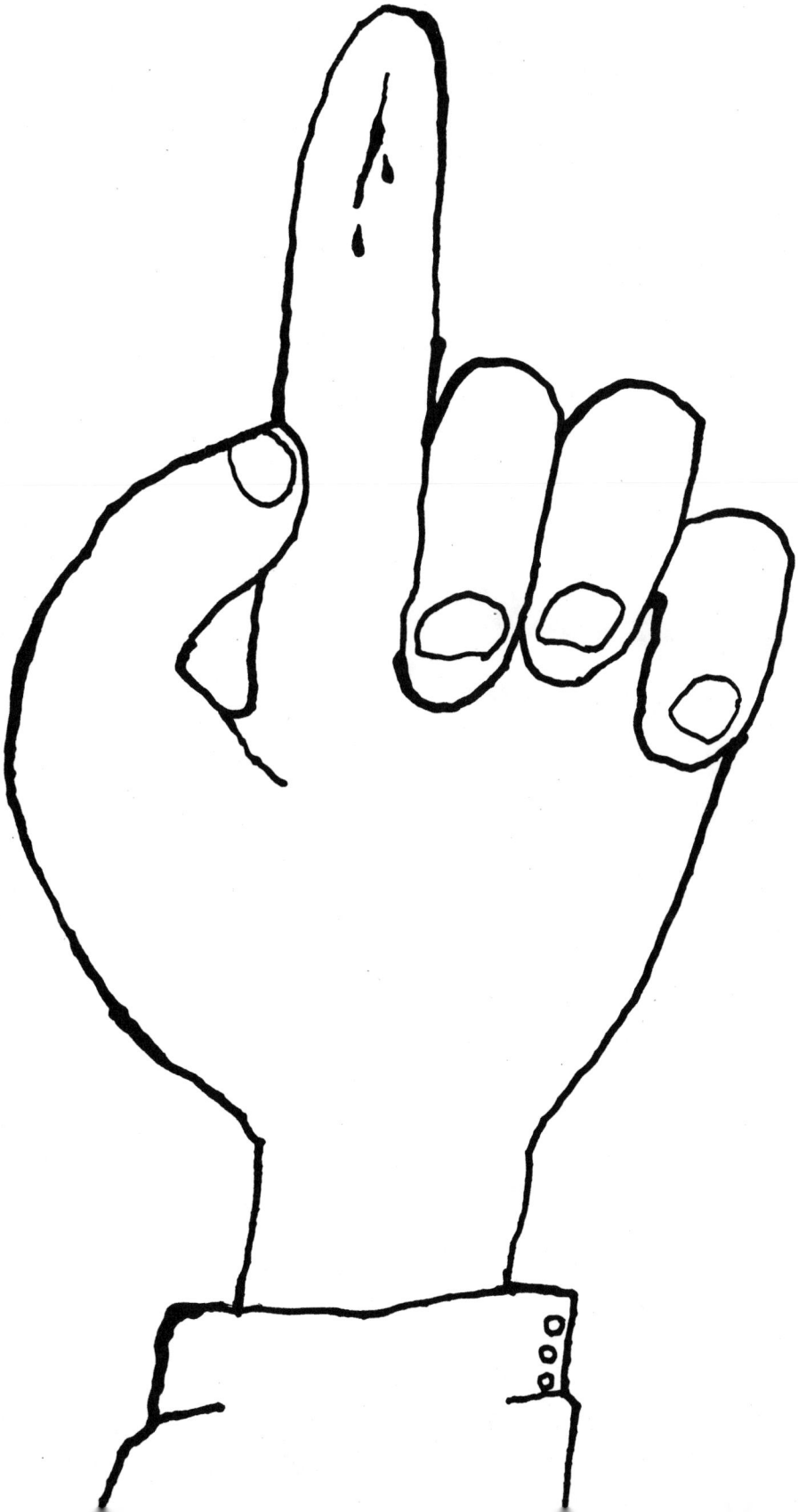

Draw some big fish

Bigger than the boat!

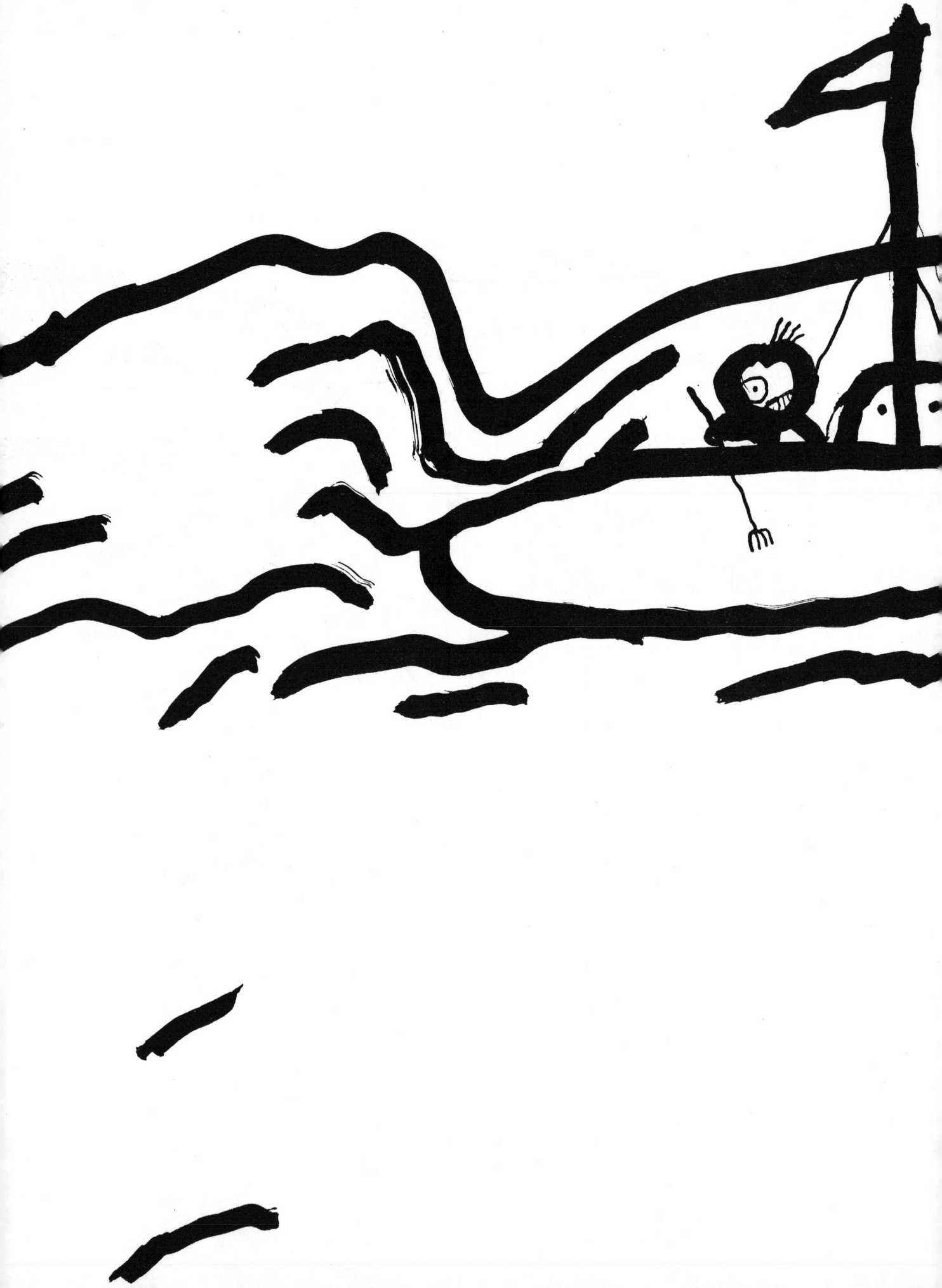

Find your way through the maze

EXIT

It's eighteen minutes to six

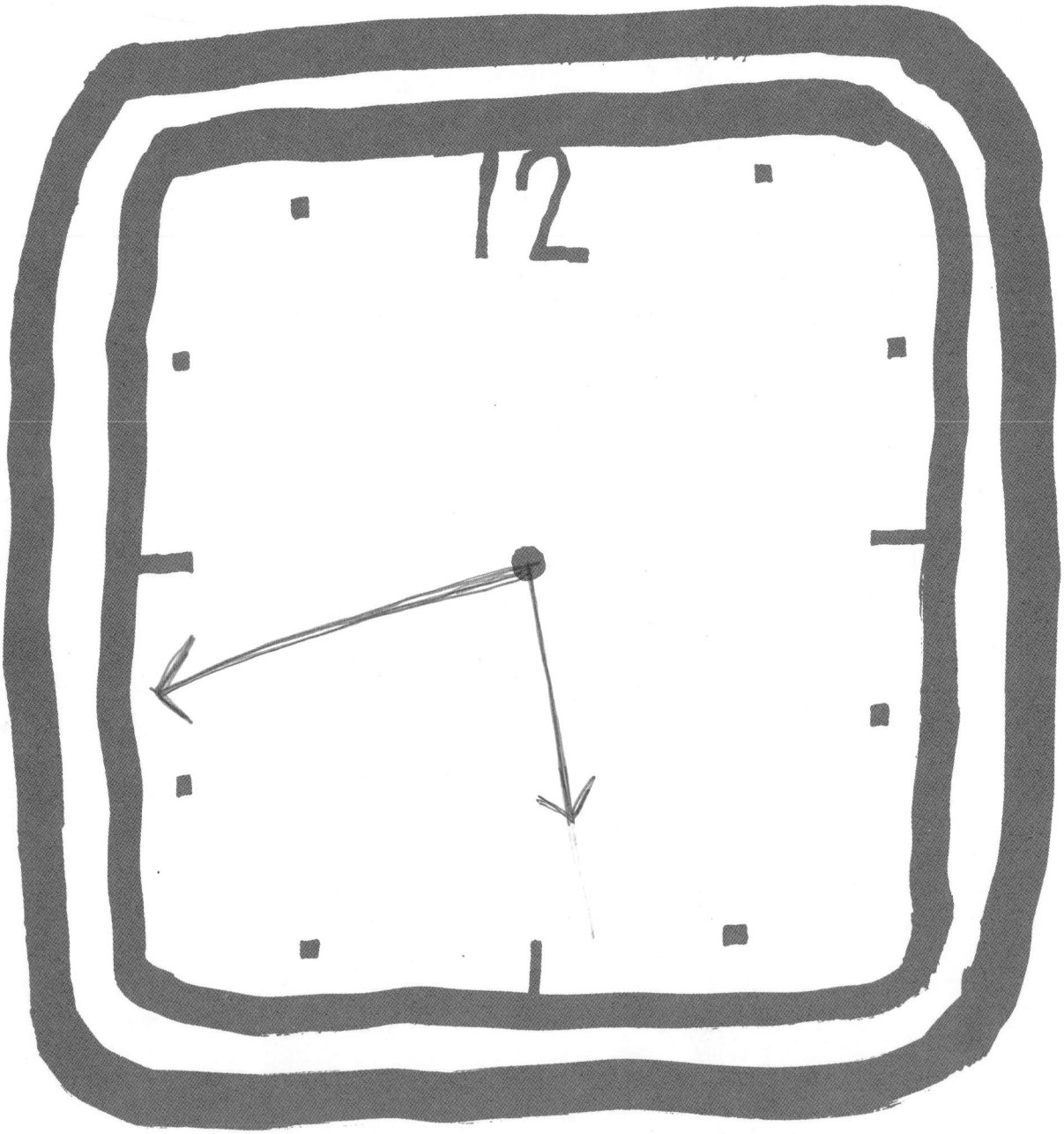

12
1
2
3
4
5
6
7
8
9
10
11
15

Draw laundry drying

BARBIE

Draw patterns on these curtains

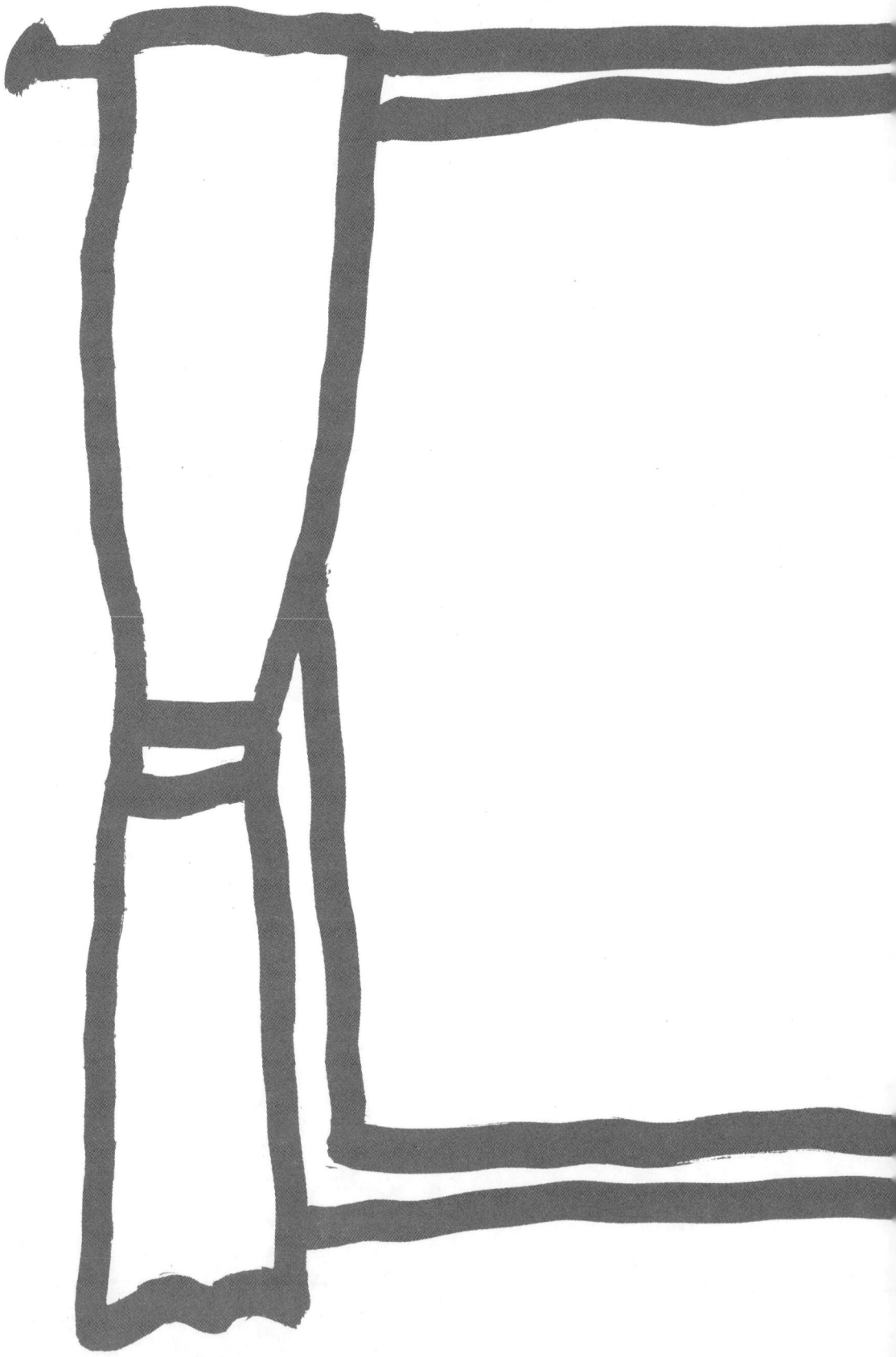

What's this?

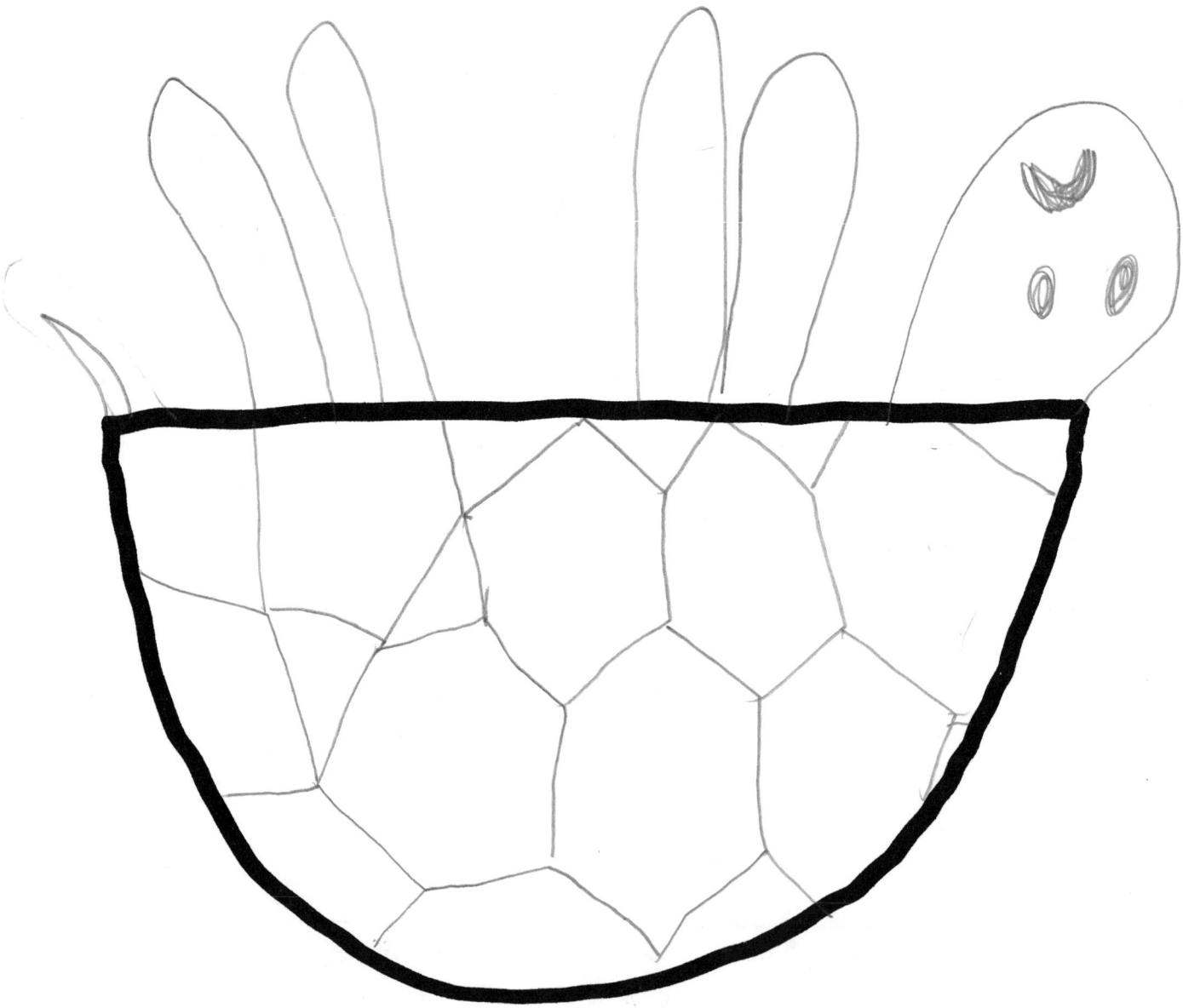

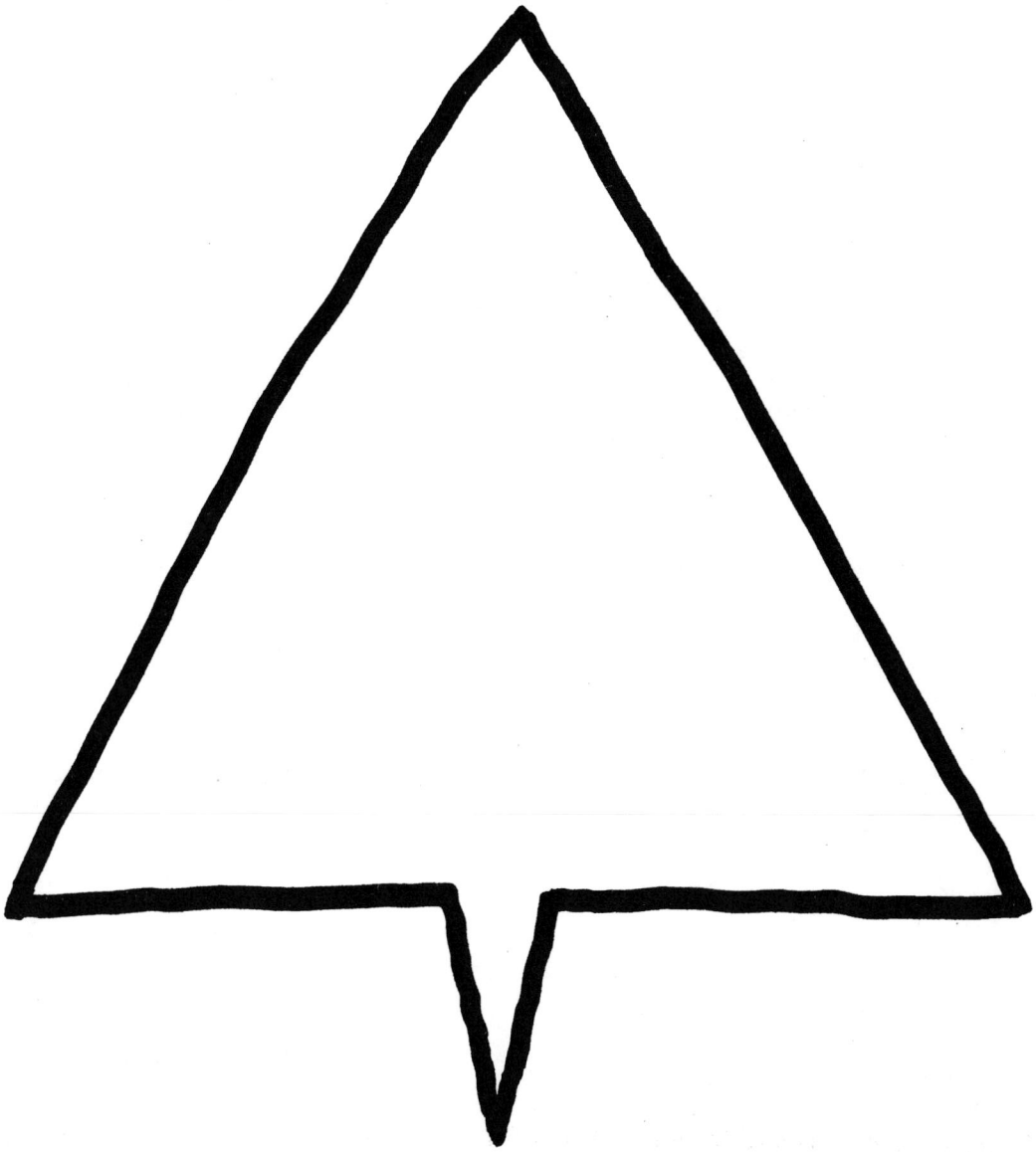

And this?

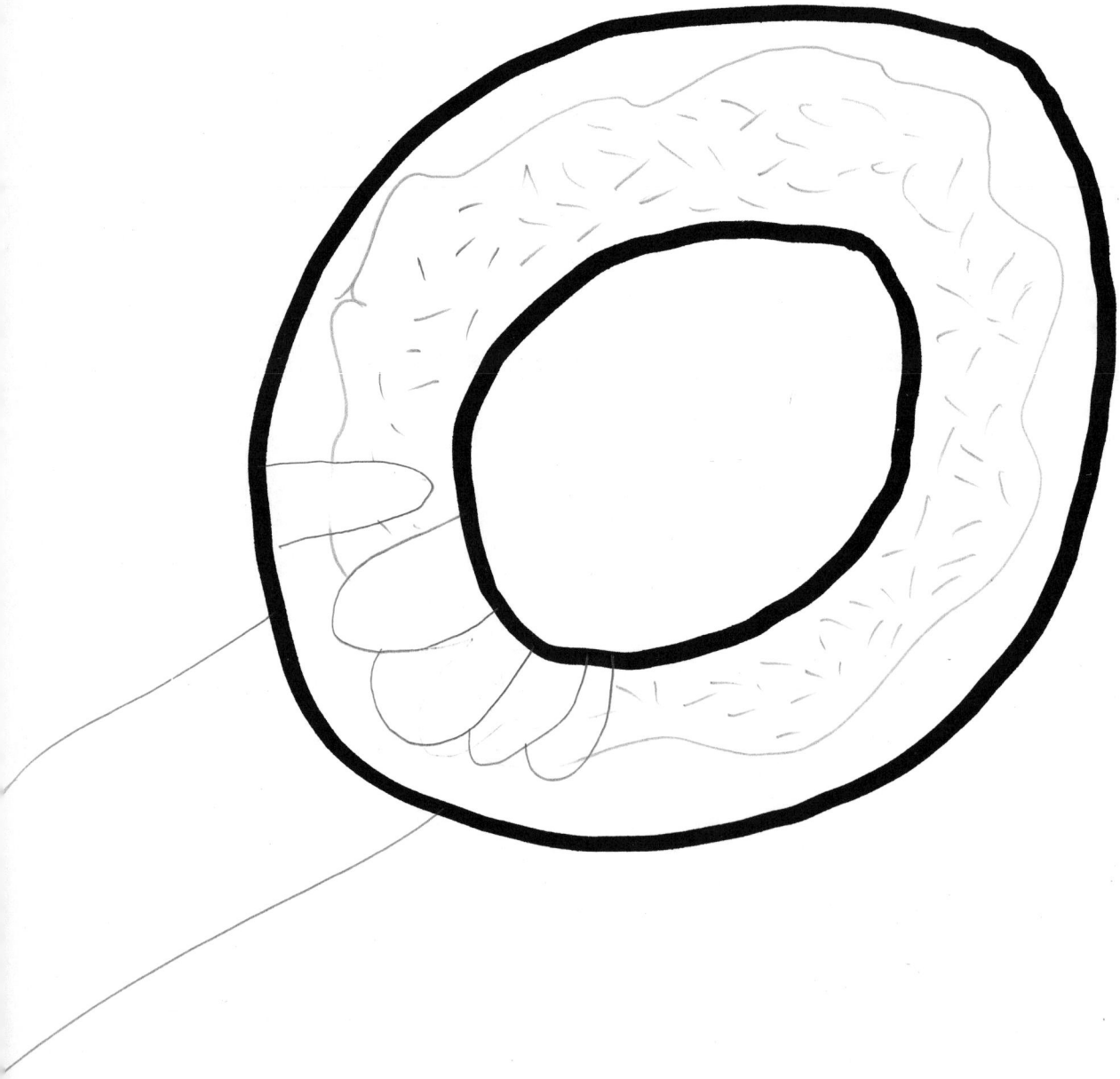

LEGO

And this?

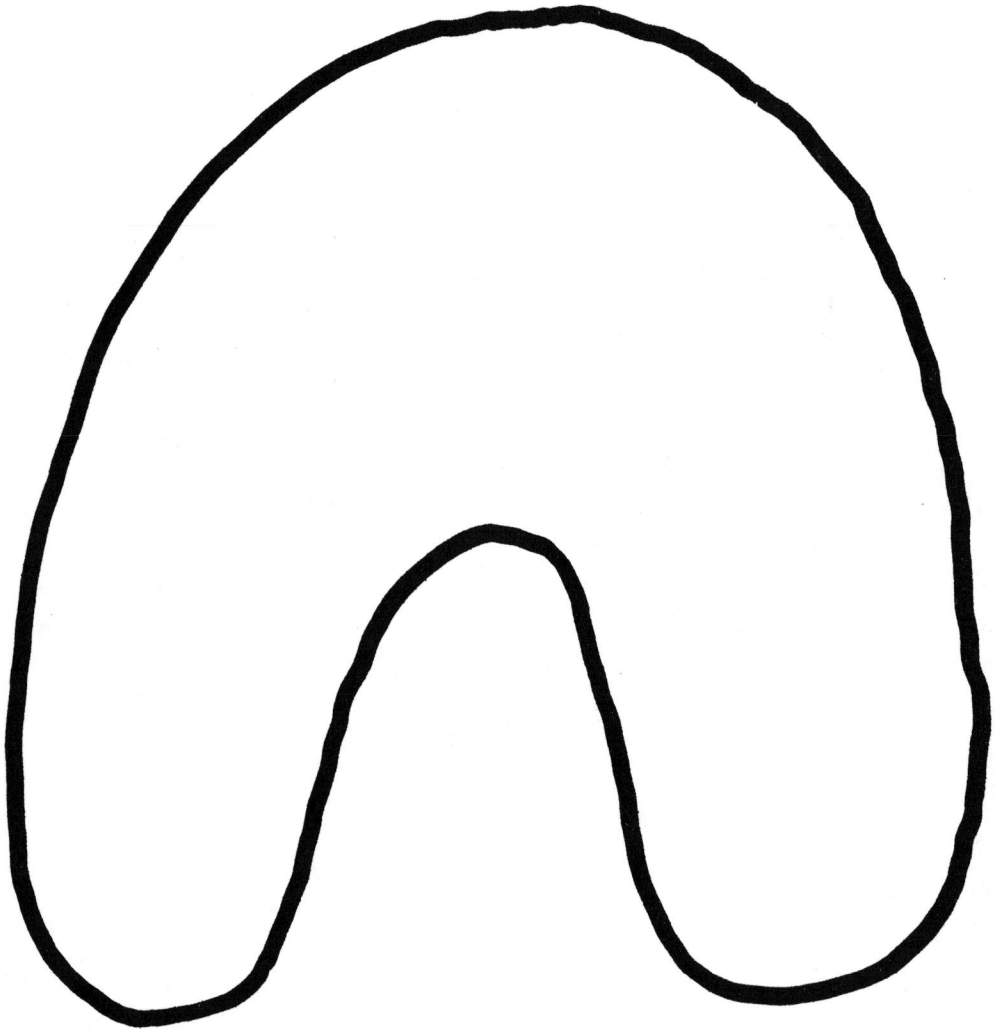

What about this?

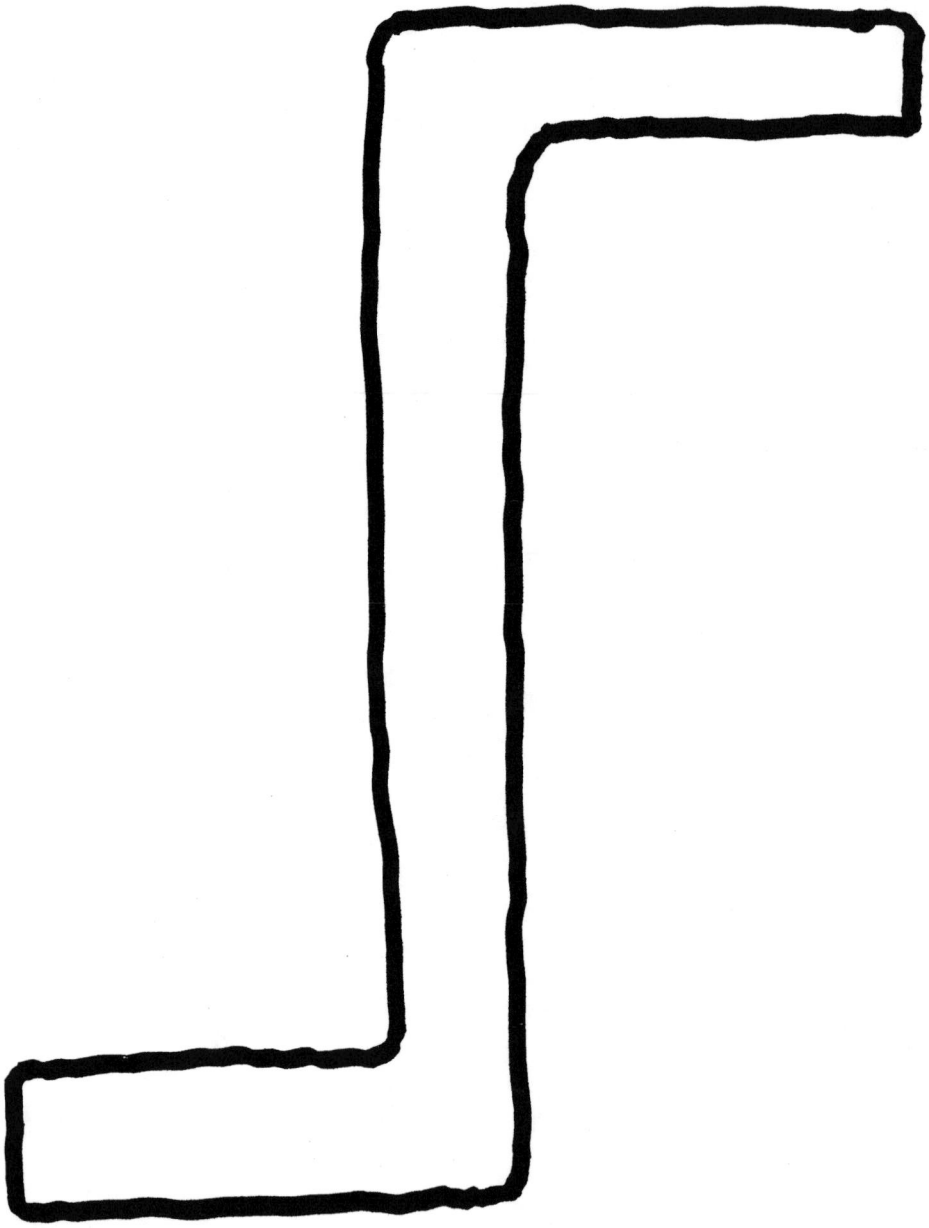

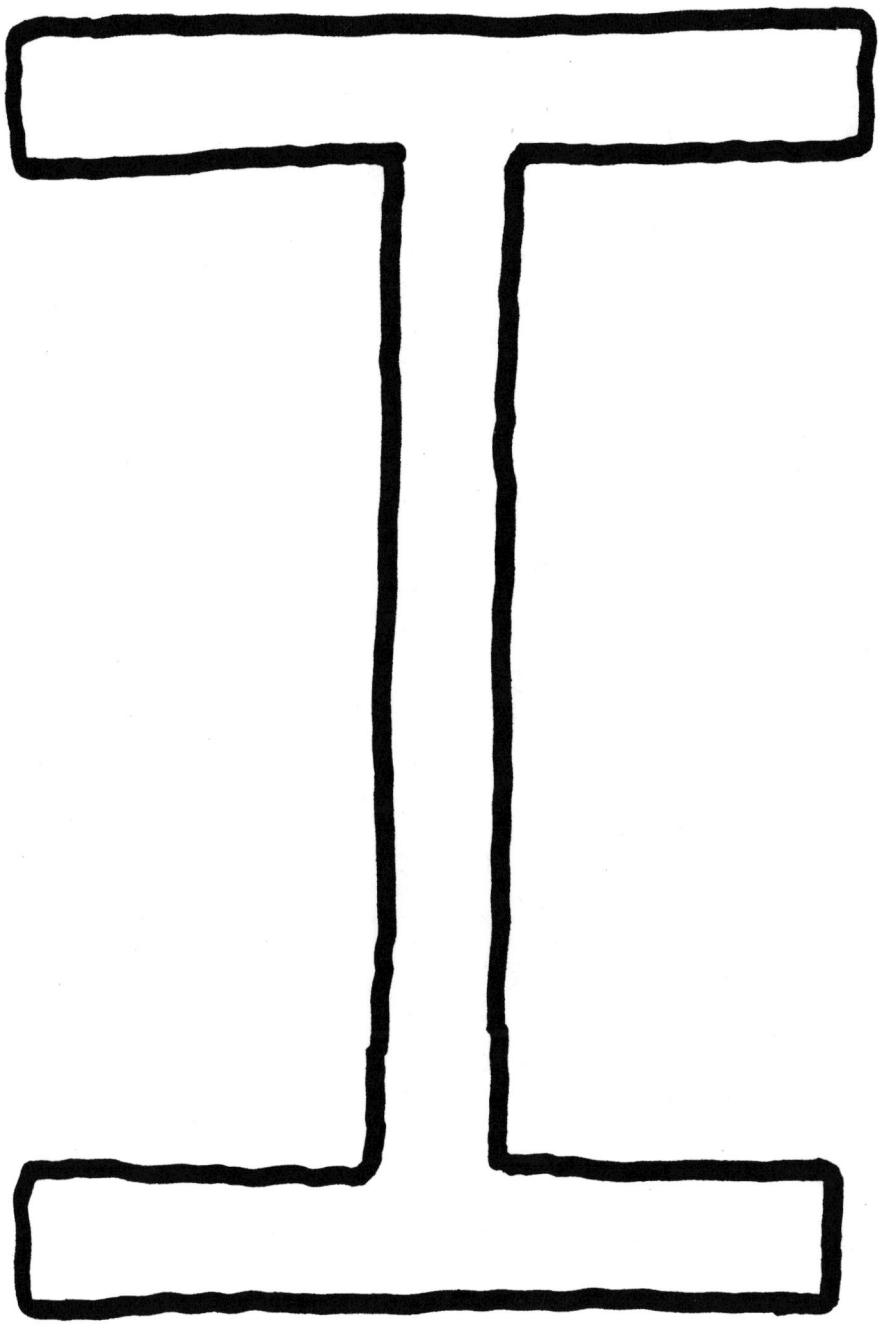

Put flowers in these vases

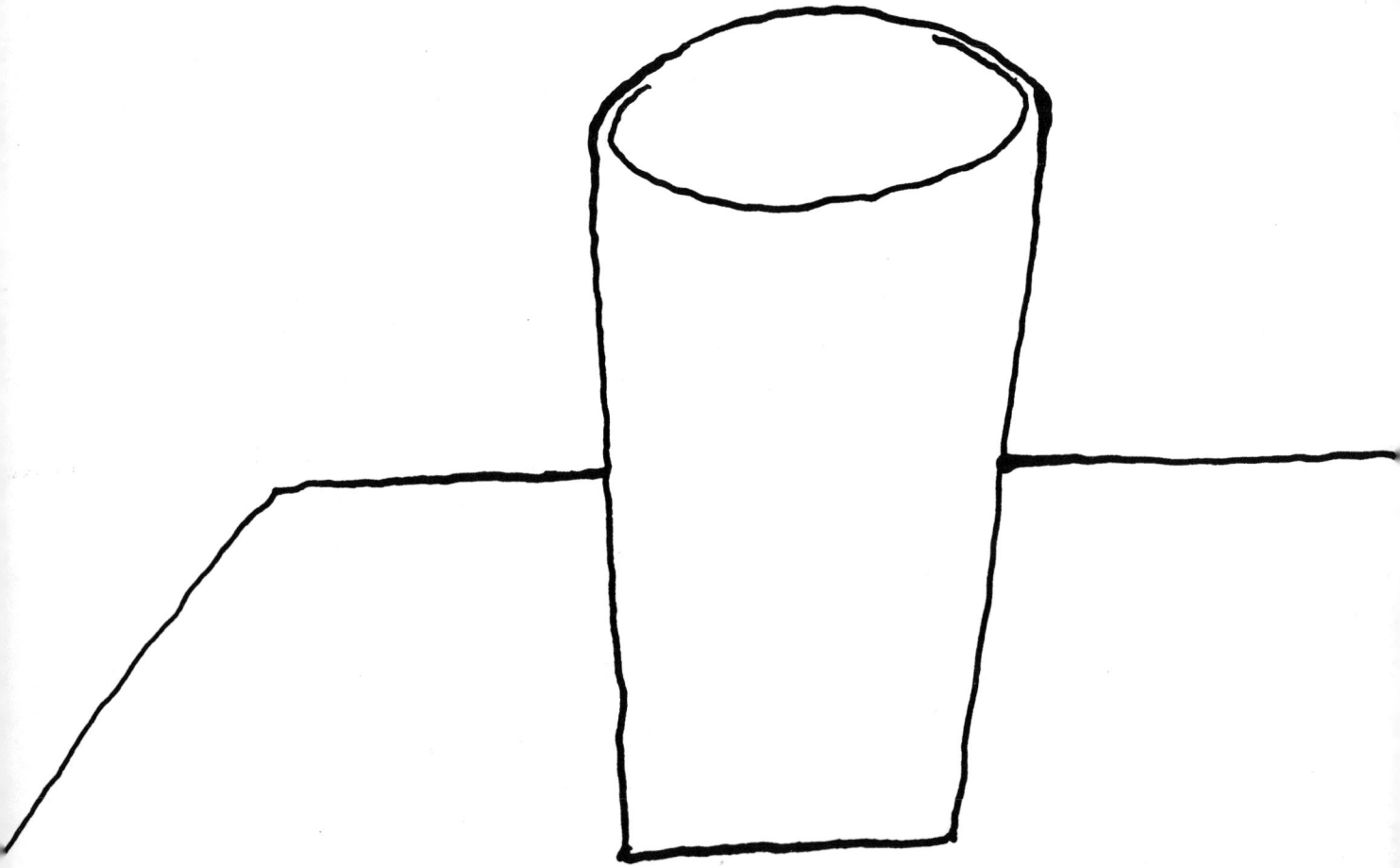

Save the little fish

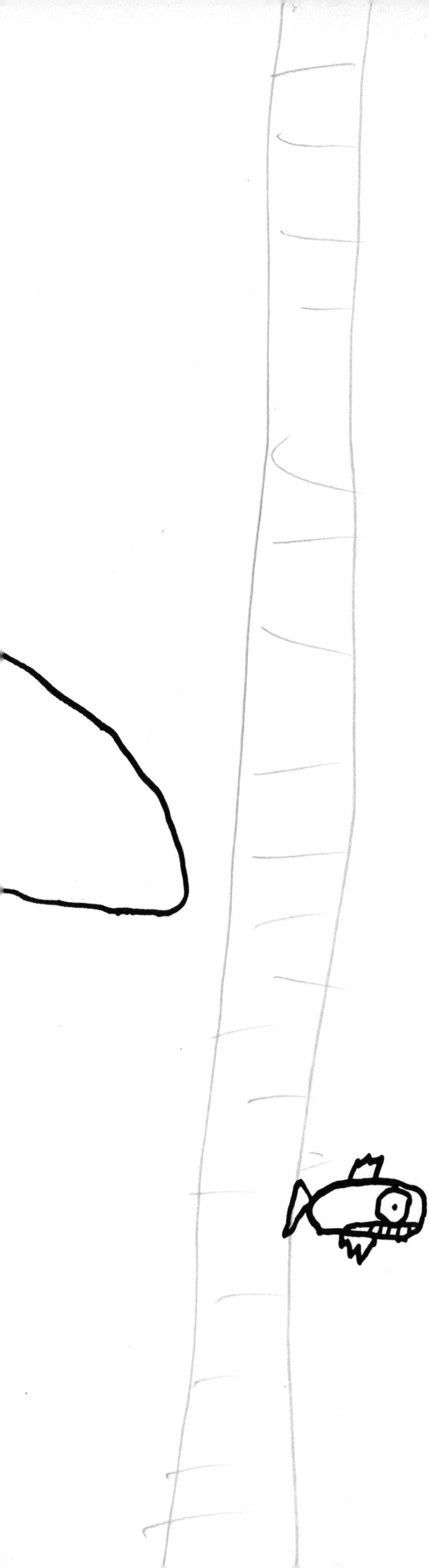

Draw a child hanging upside down

Draw someone on the swing

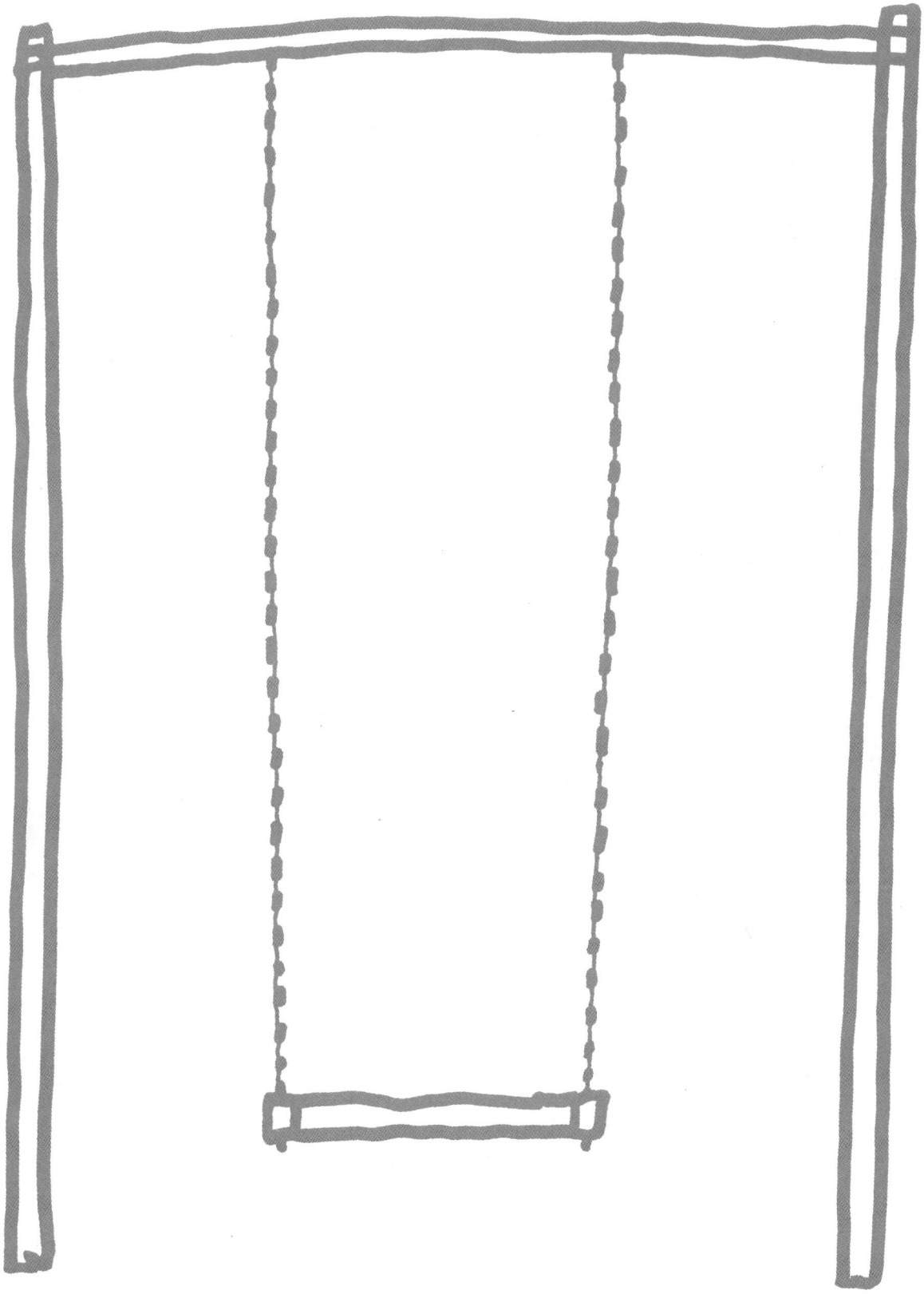

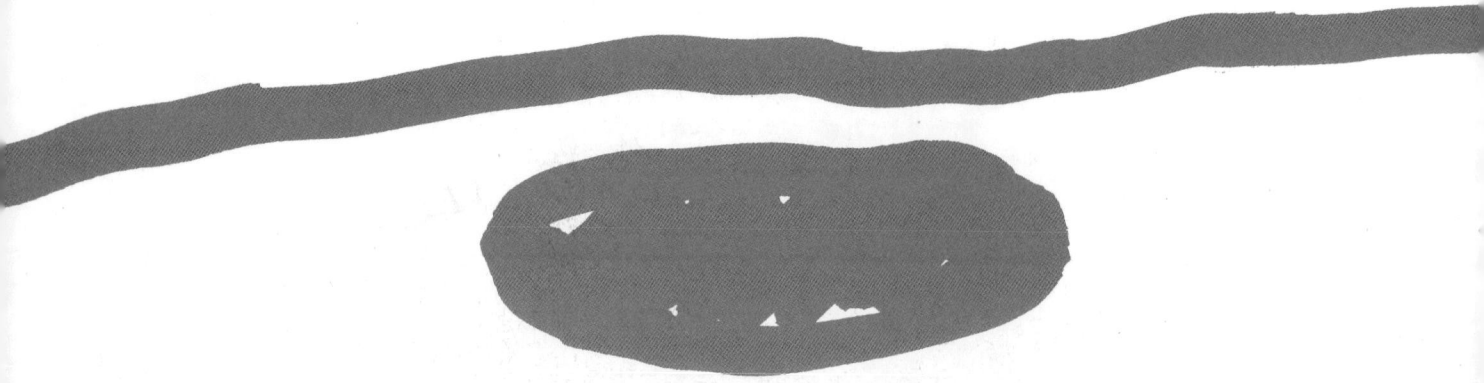

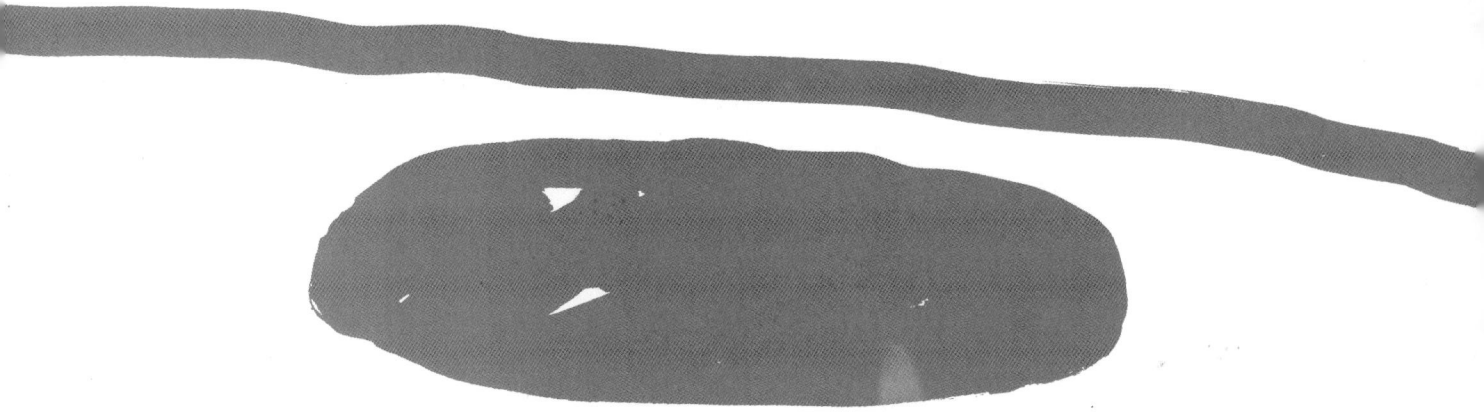

Yikes! A cockroach!

Draw a chick hatching

Now draw a chick that hasn't hatched yet

Watch out! Water's coming out of the hose!

Draw the vapor trail behind this plane

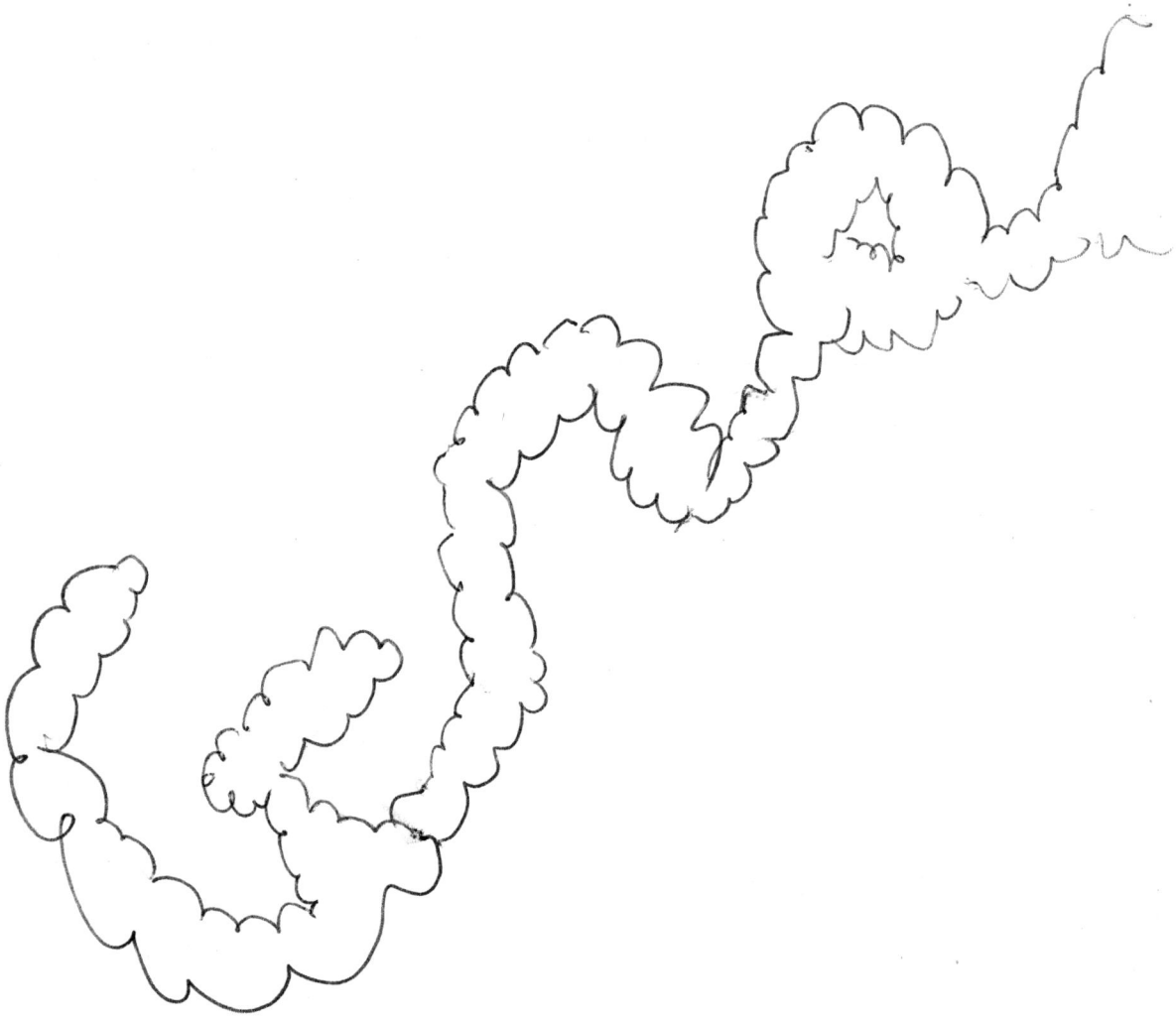

Draw the fish that I just caught

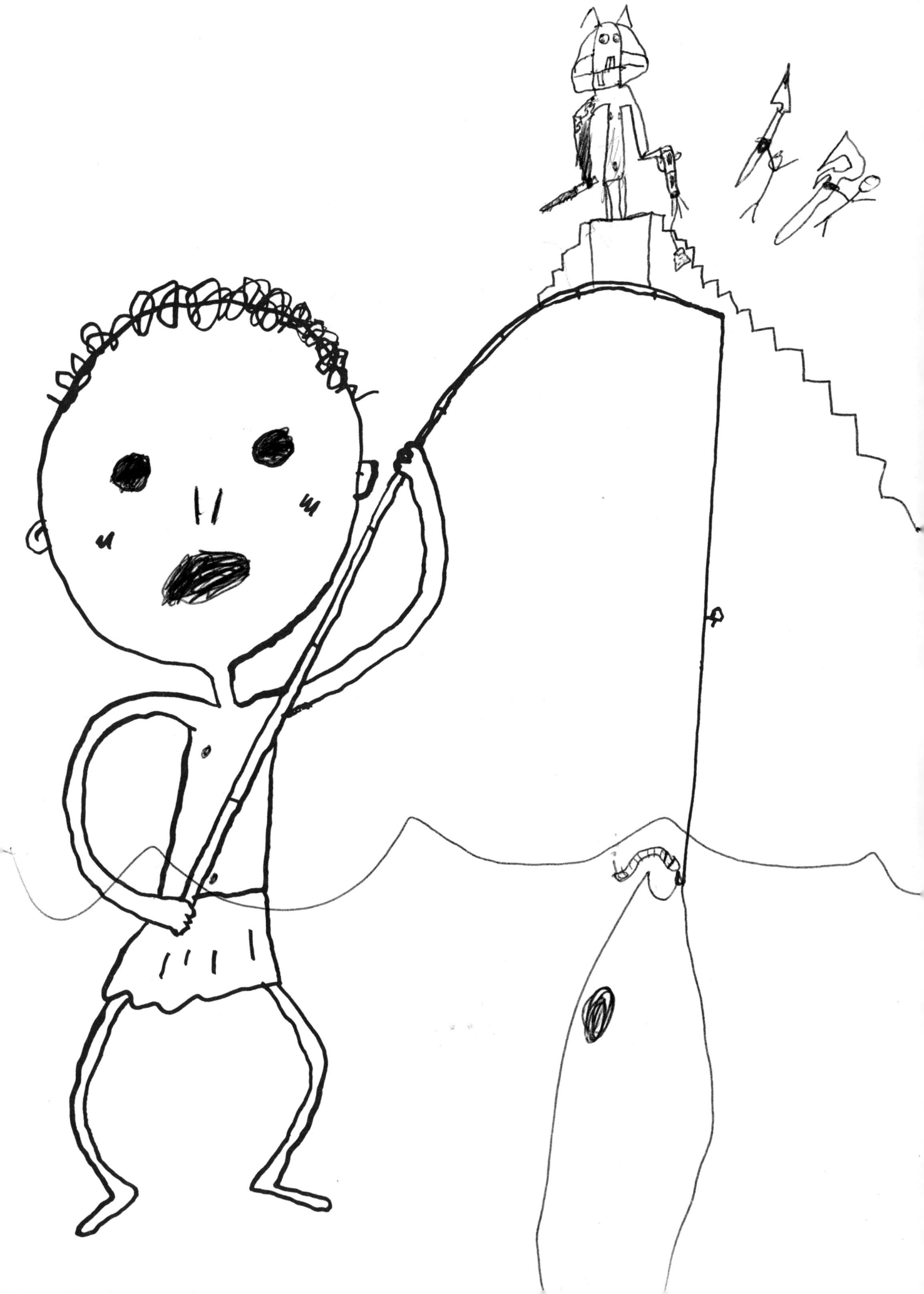

Draw a goldfish

What are they saying?

What are they saying?

You're too Pretty!!
You're too Ugly!!

What are they saying?

Hmph.
I LOVE FIGHT.
I'm gonna tell my mamma on YOU!

The passengers are throwing confetti

These animals have polka dots

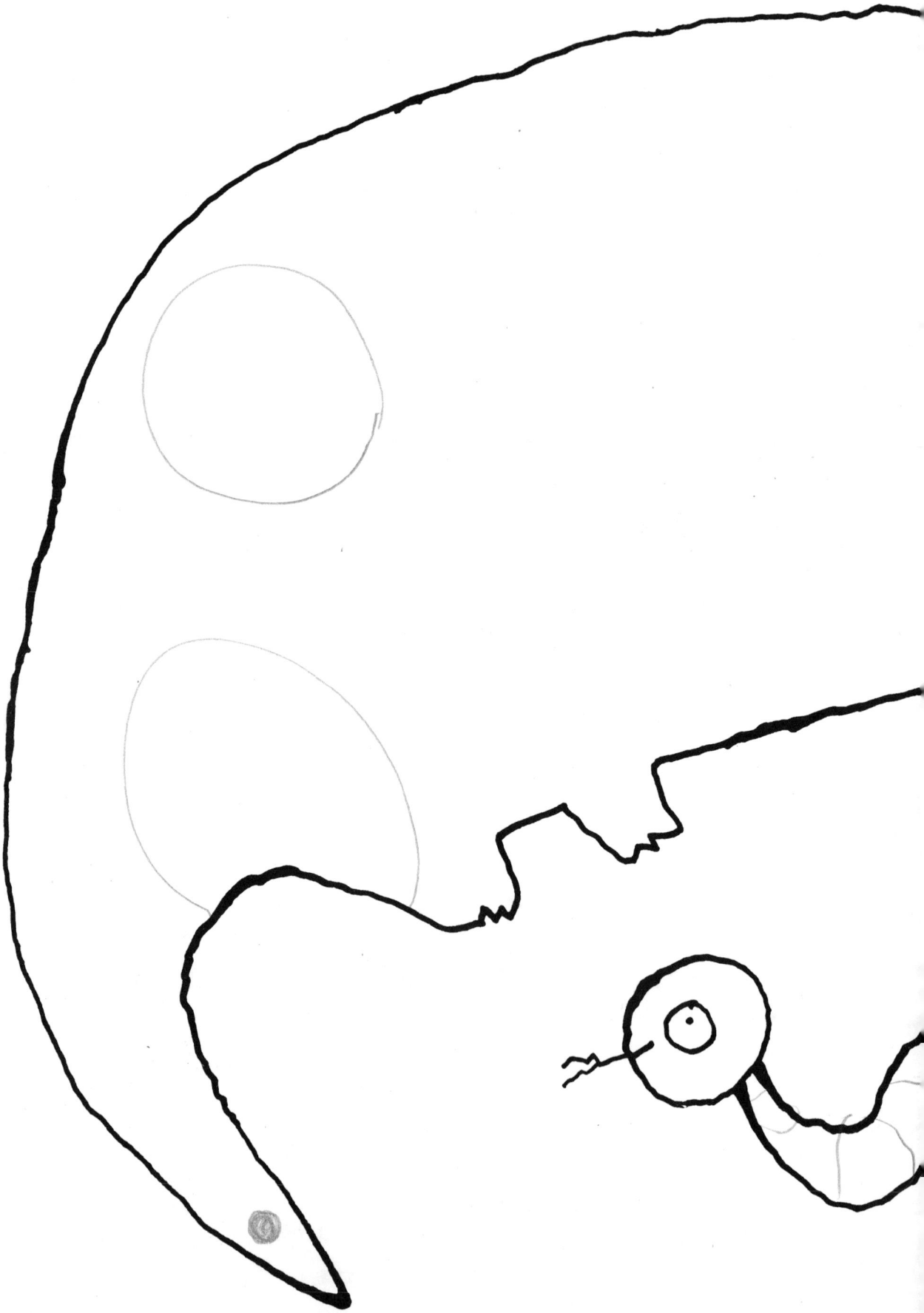

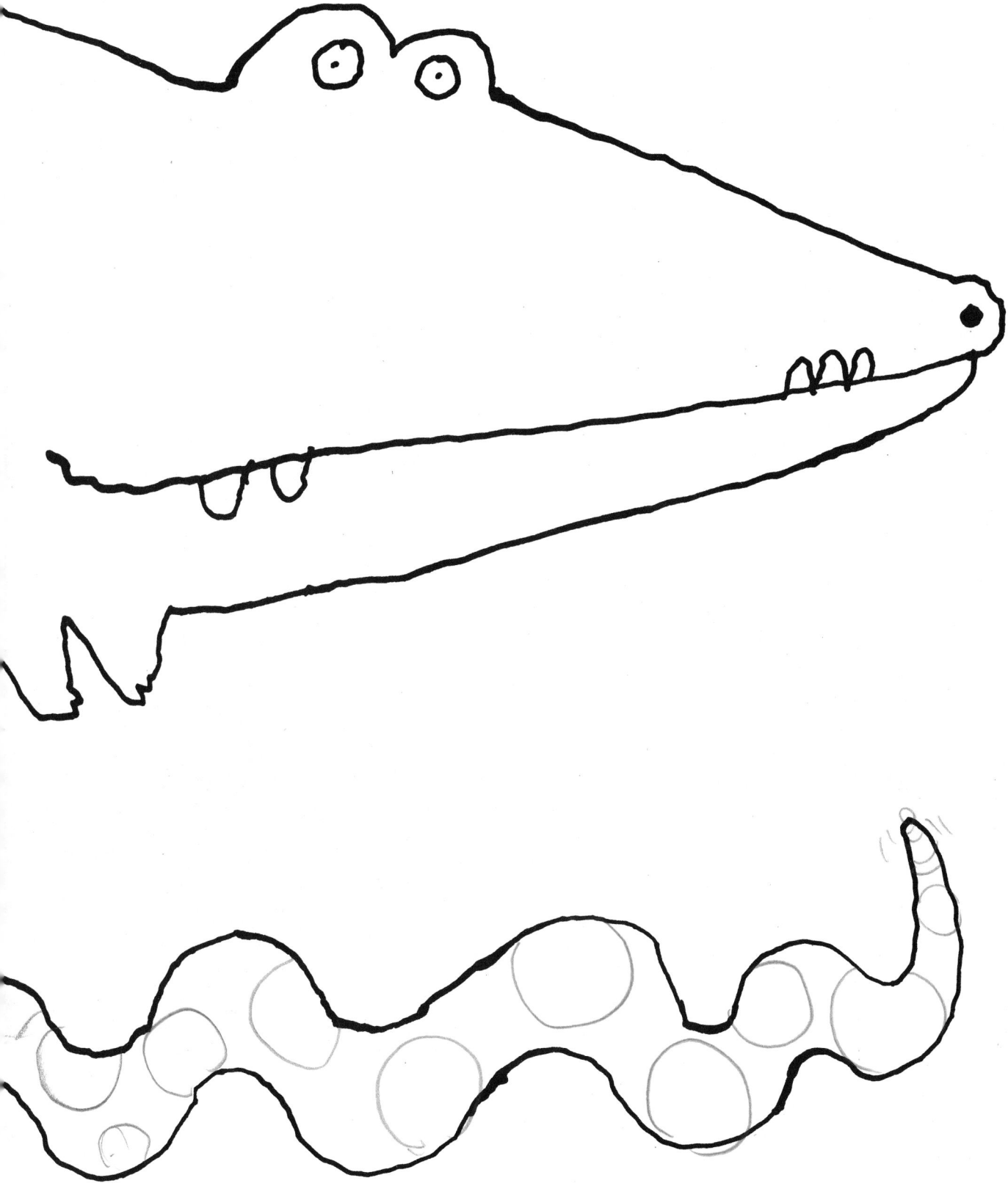

Attack the monster

Make him disappear by covering him completely

Help the bunny find his way

Draw a TV show you really like

What color is the mouse?

What color is the elephant?

Draw people swimming

Color this bear black

Color this bear white

Whew! It's hot!

Color the thermometer

Brrr! It's cold!

Draw power lines

This crocodile is in a bad mood

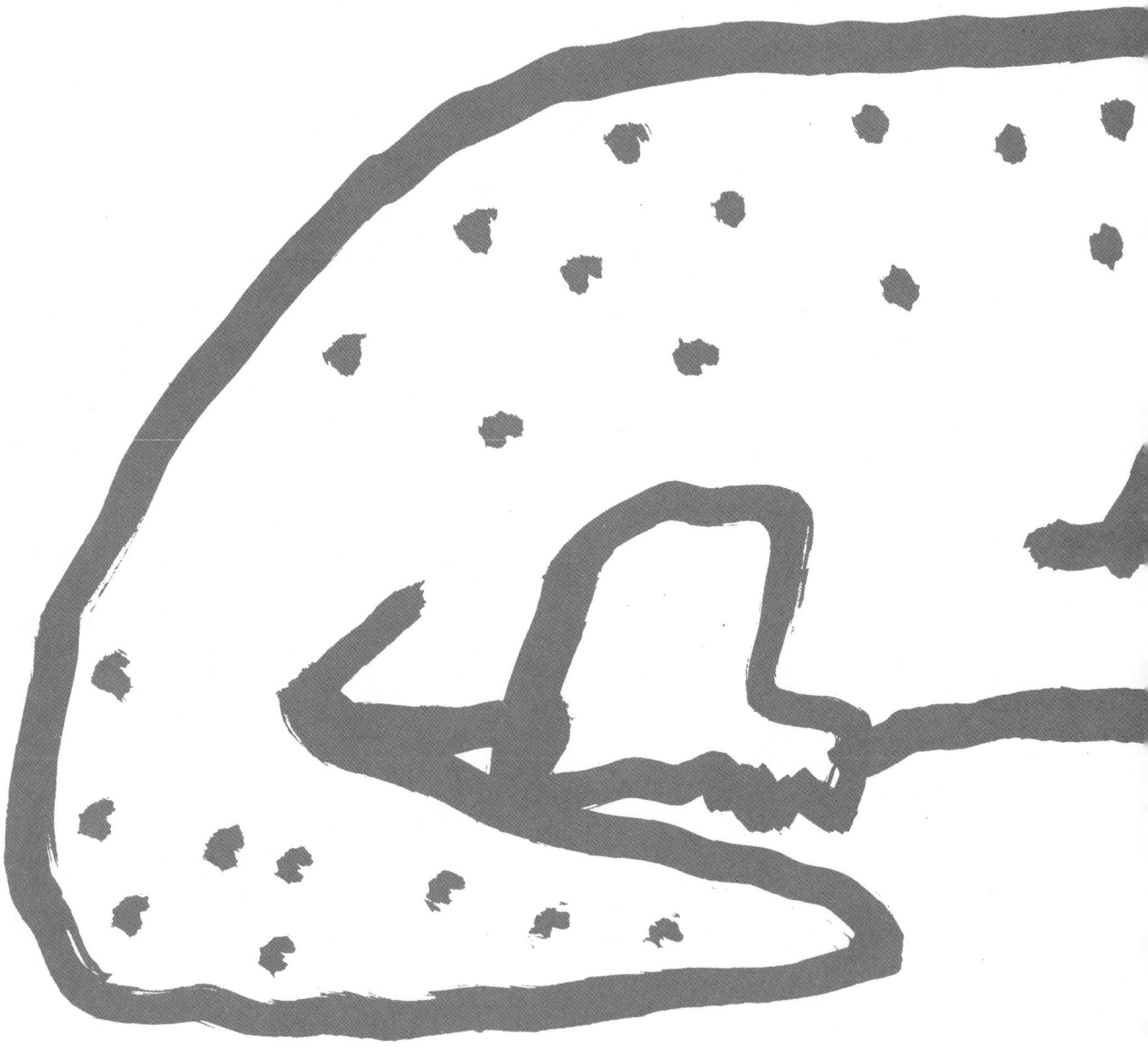

Draw a pot or a tea kettle

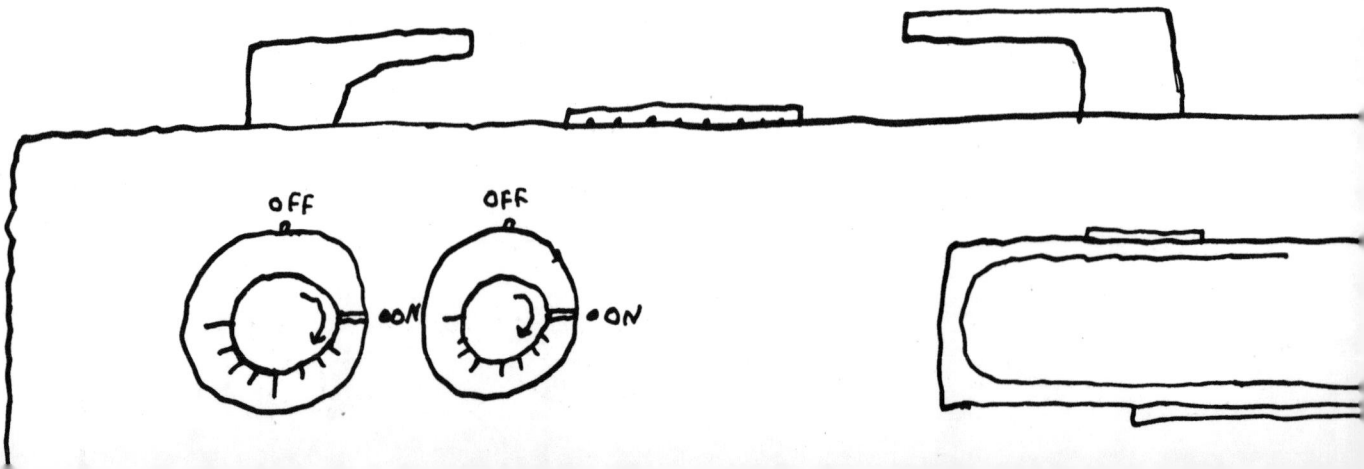

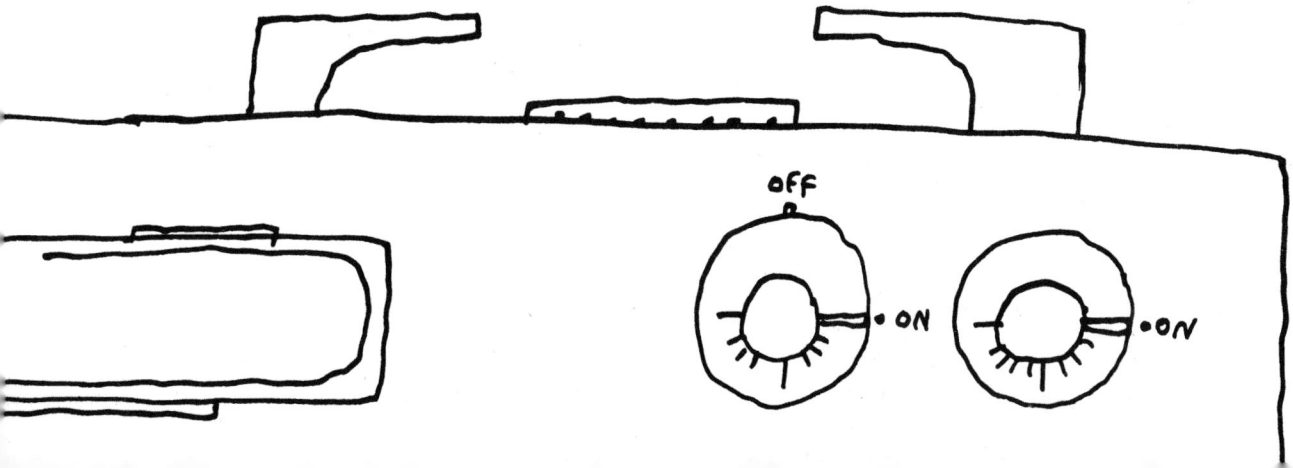
OFF
ON
ON

Color 7 apples

Color 10 apples

Color the blocks

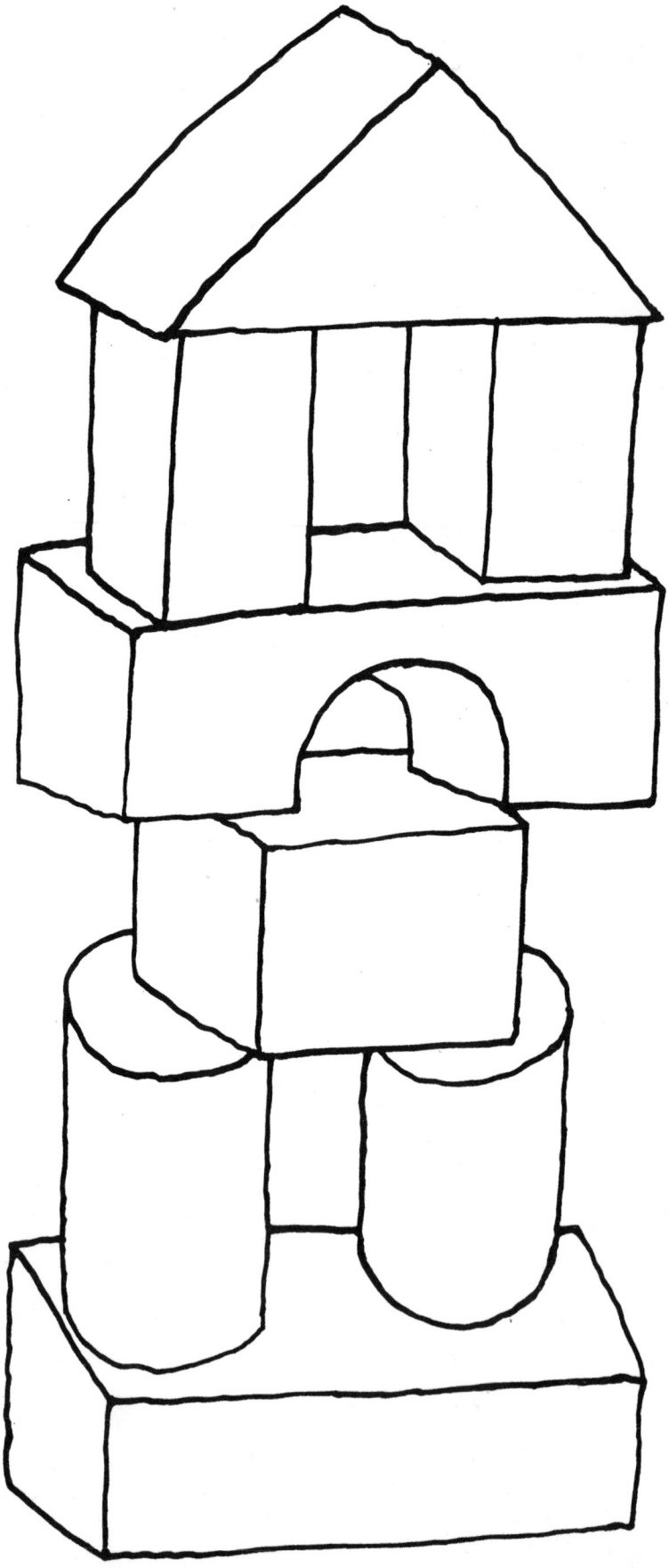

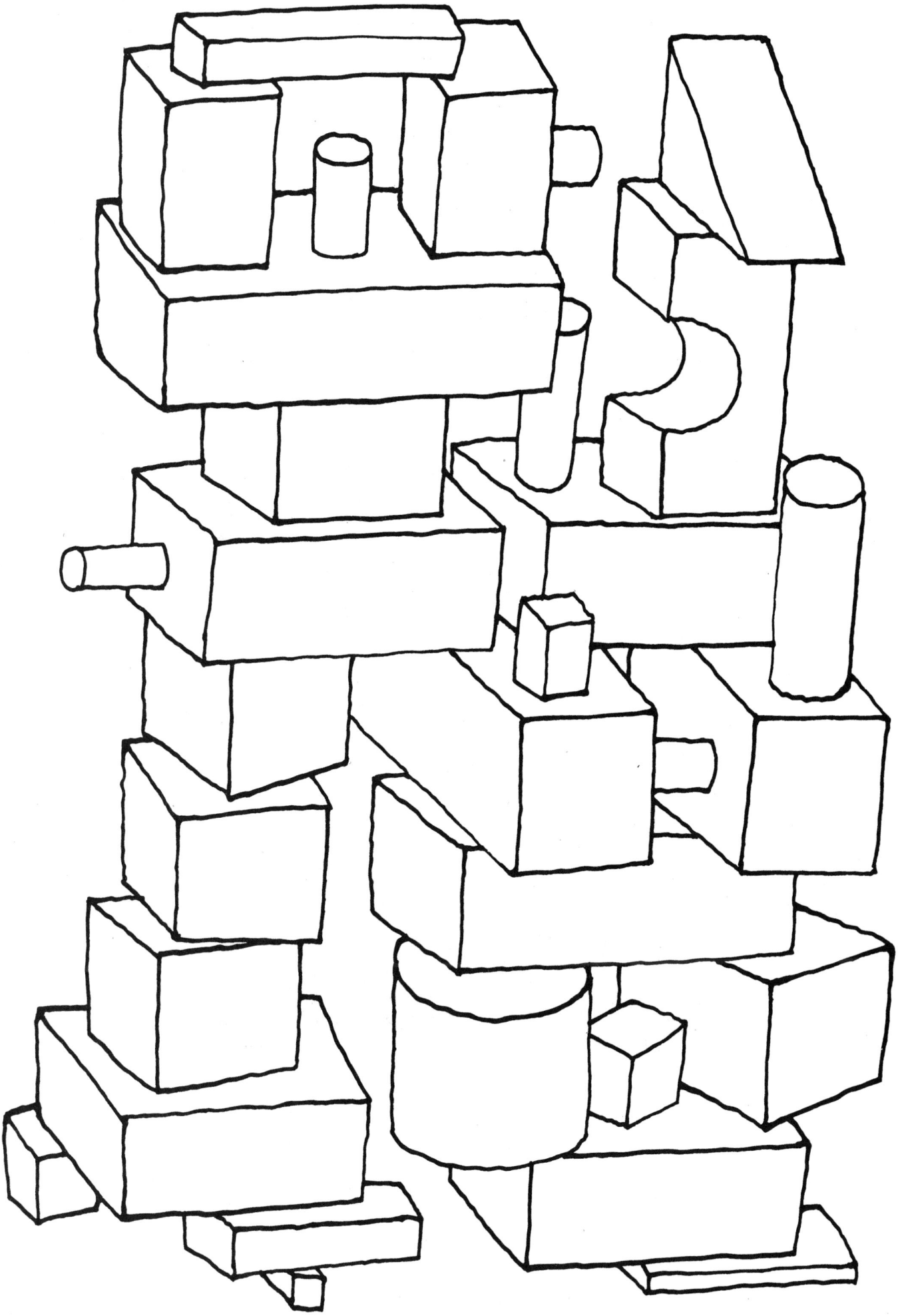

This is a mountain of sugar

Draw ants marching

Draw babies

Make them as cute as you can

Draw a racecourse around these flags

Go around all of the flags

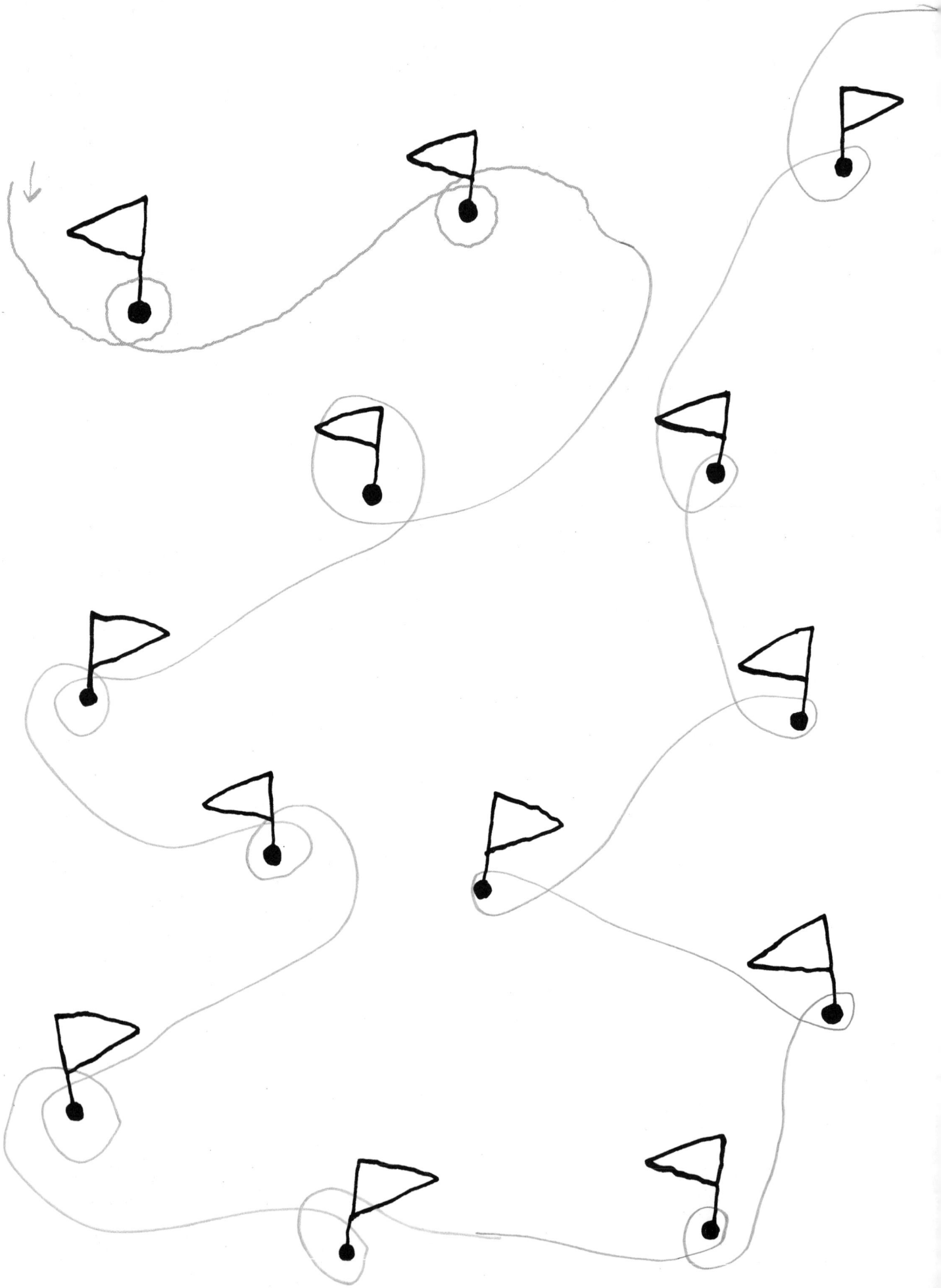

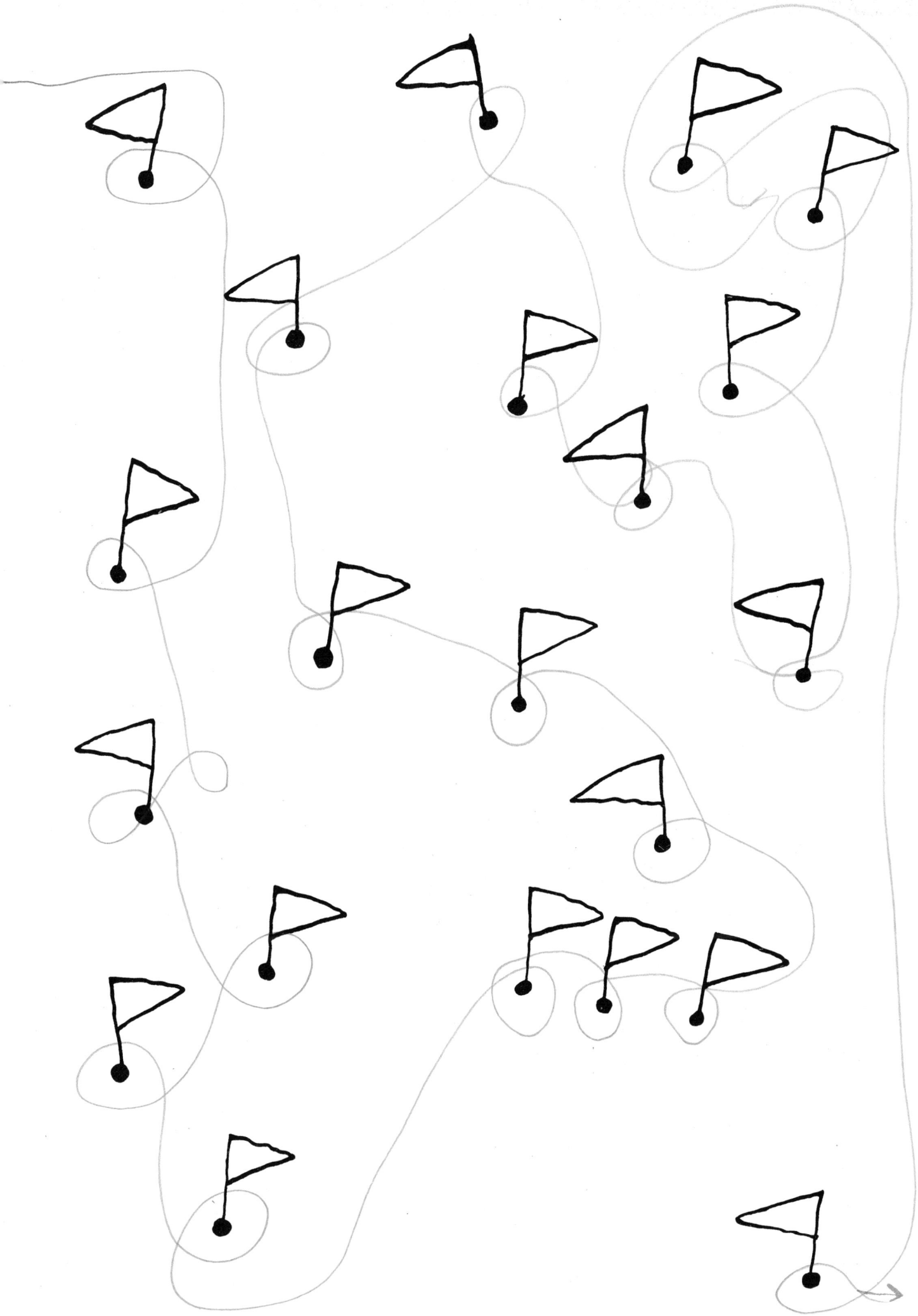

It's Christmas!

Decorate the tree and light the candle

Draw 2 clowns

One on the ball and one on the horse

Draw some ducks on this pond

This penguin is very cold

How can you warm him up?

This owl is very tired

Draw him a bed to sleep in

Draw their glasses

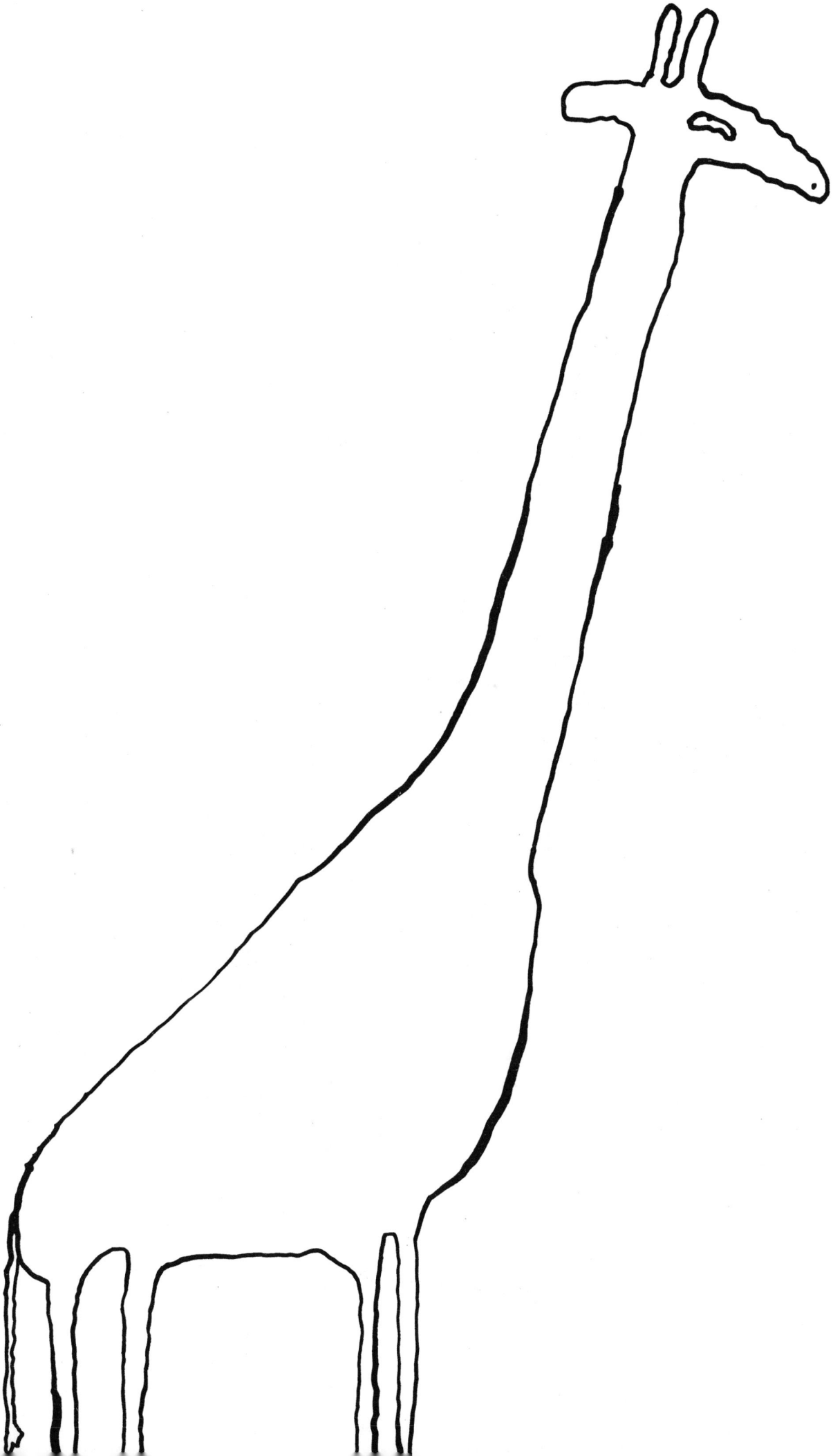

Draw something in each box

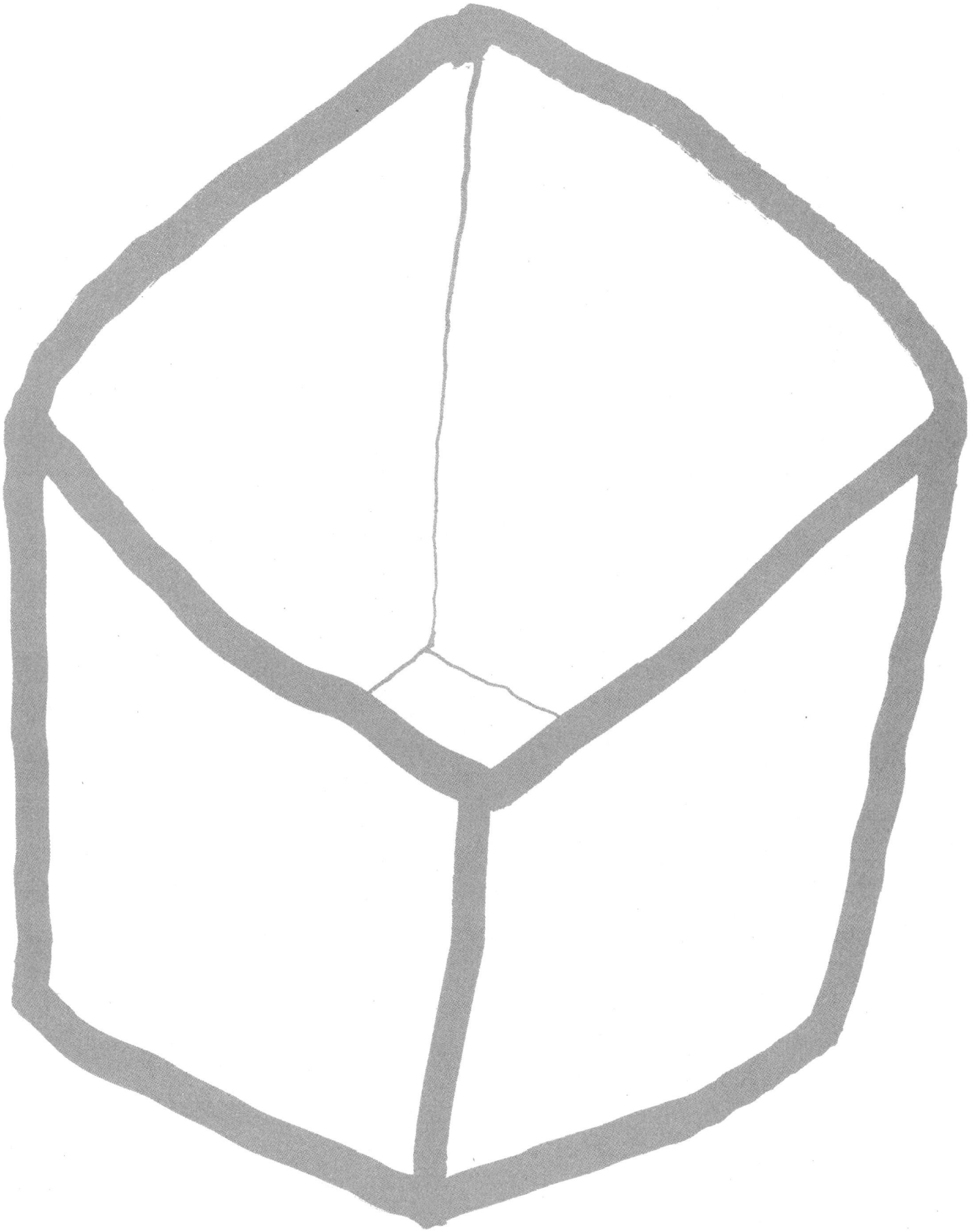

Color 36 cherries

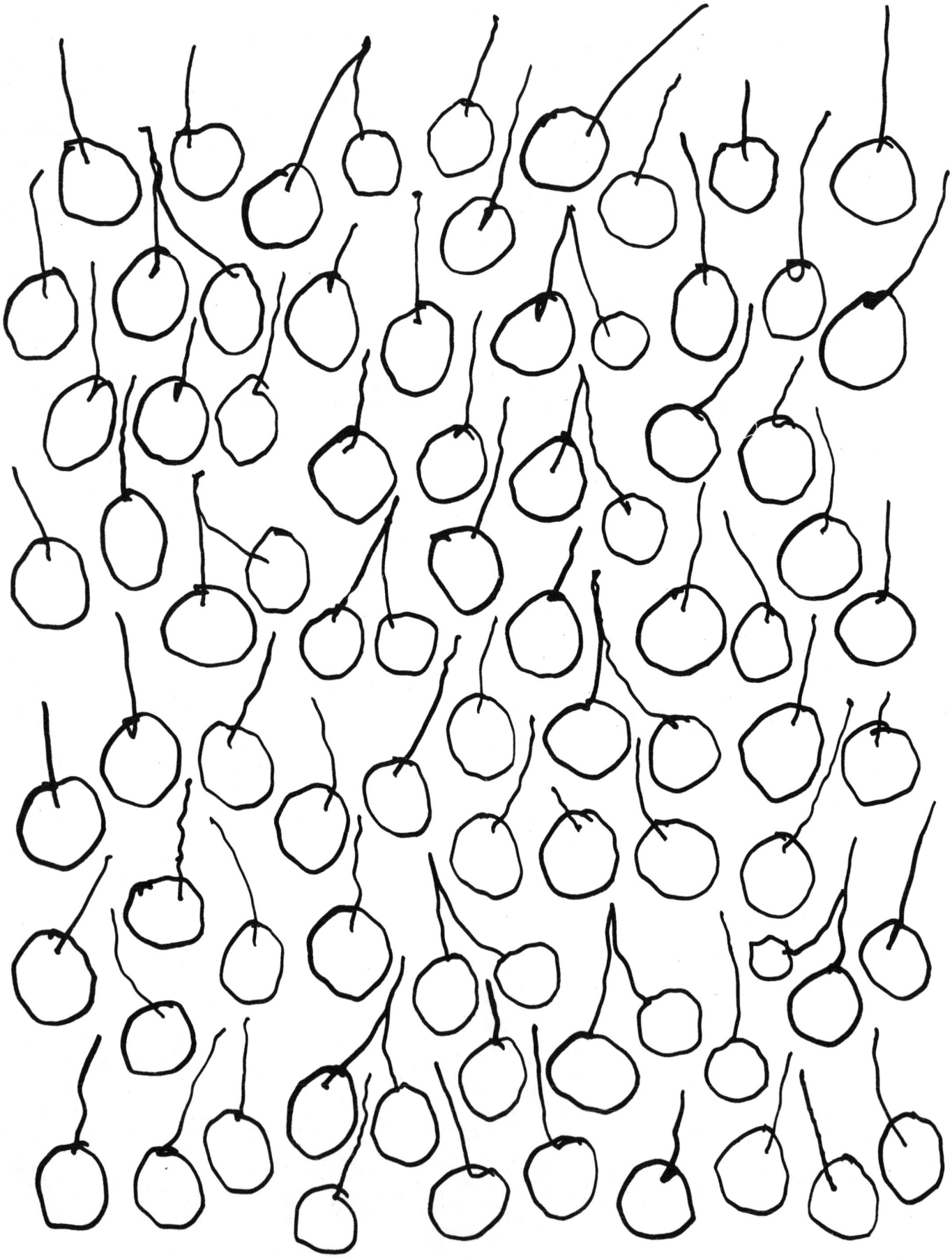

Color 632 of them

Hang in there!

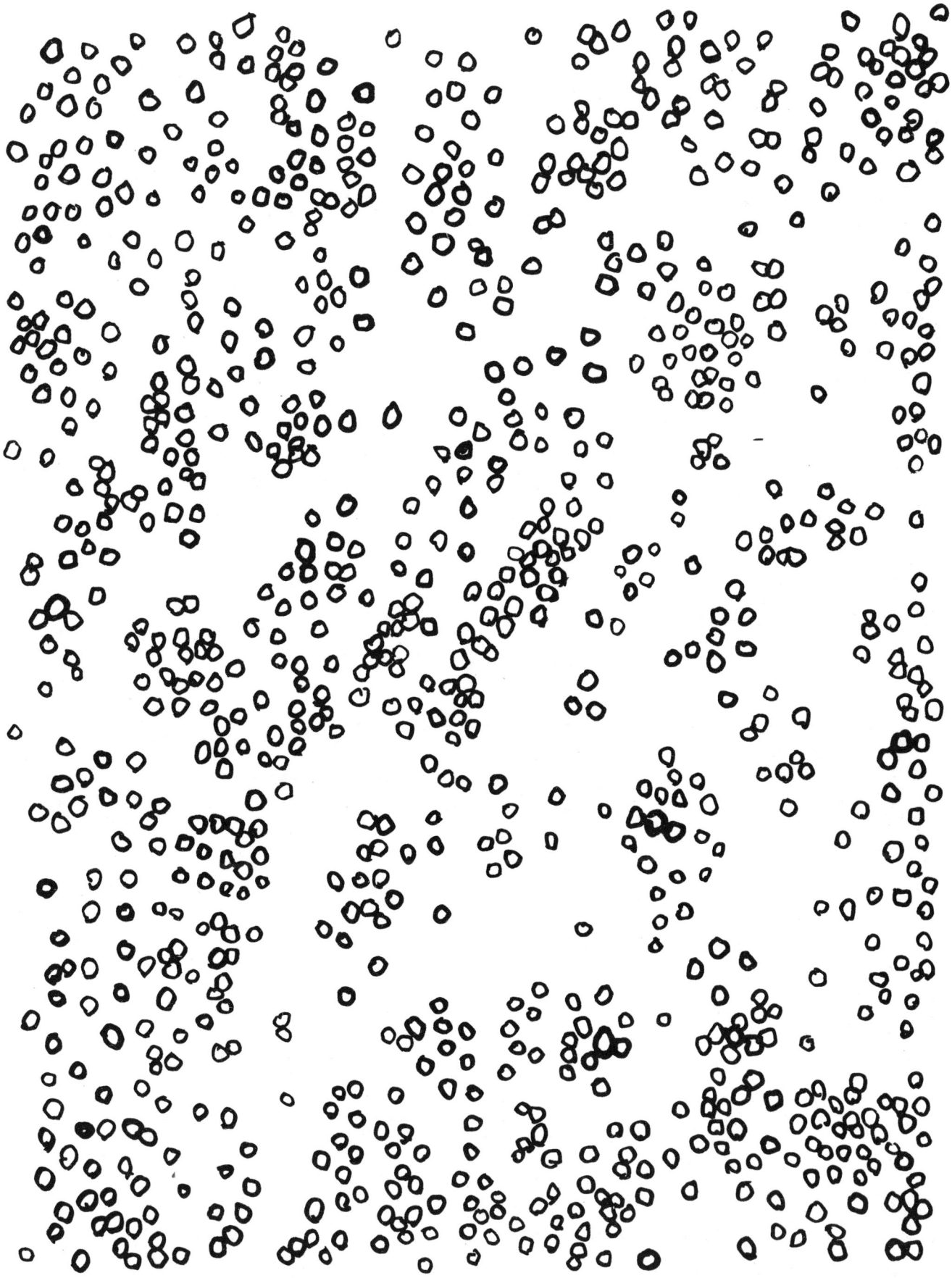

Draw ads on these billboards

NEW
Speakeasy
RoadStar
HINOKIYA MOTOR COMPANY LIMITED.
空売王
さるがしストアー
あなたも3日で国際人!!
HOW ARE YOU
英会話学院
生徒募

Draw faces

Make these two look more friendly

Draw ribbons on these presents

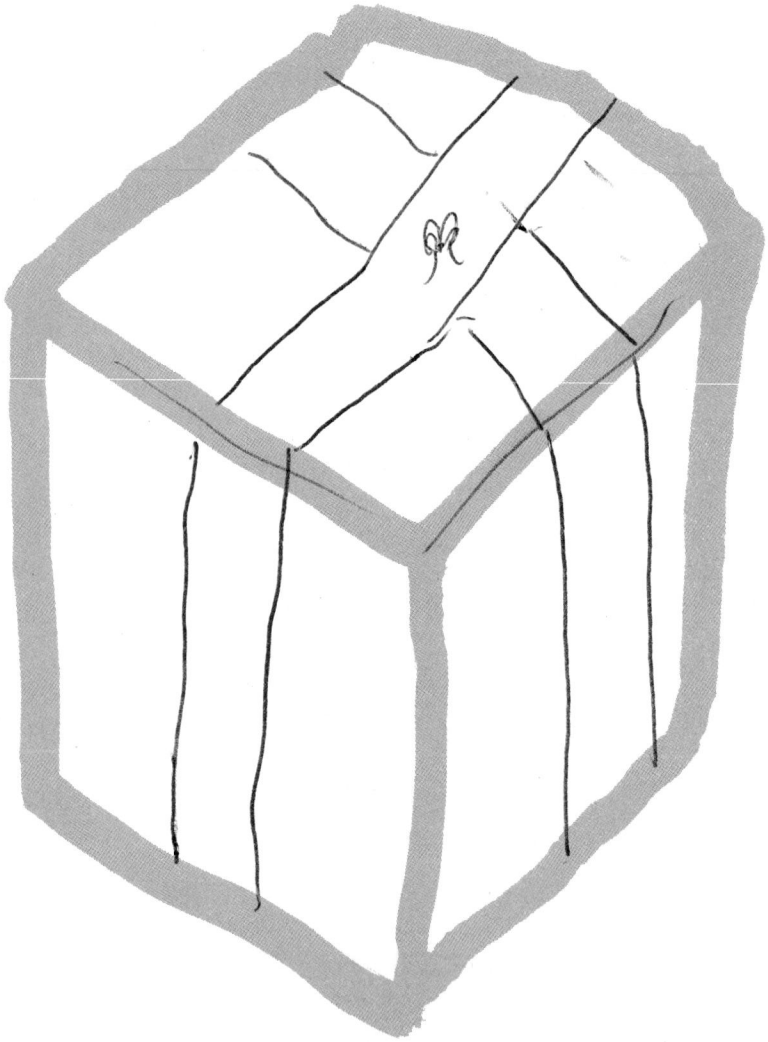

Draw a few more astronauts

Draw the animals in the zoo

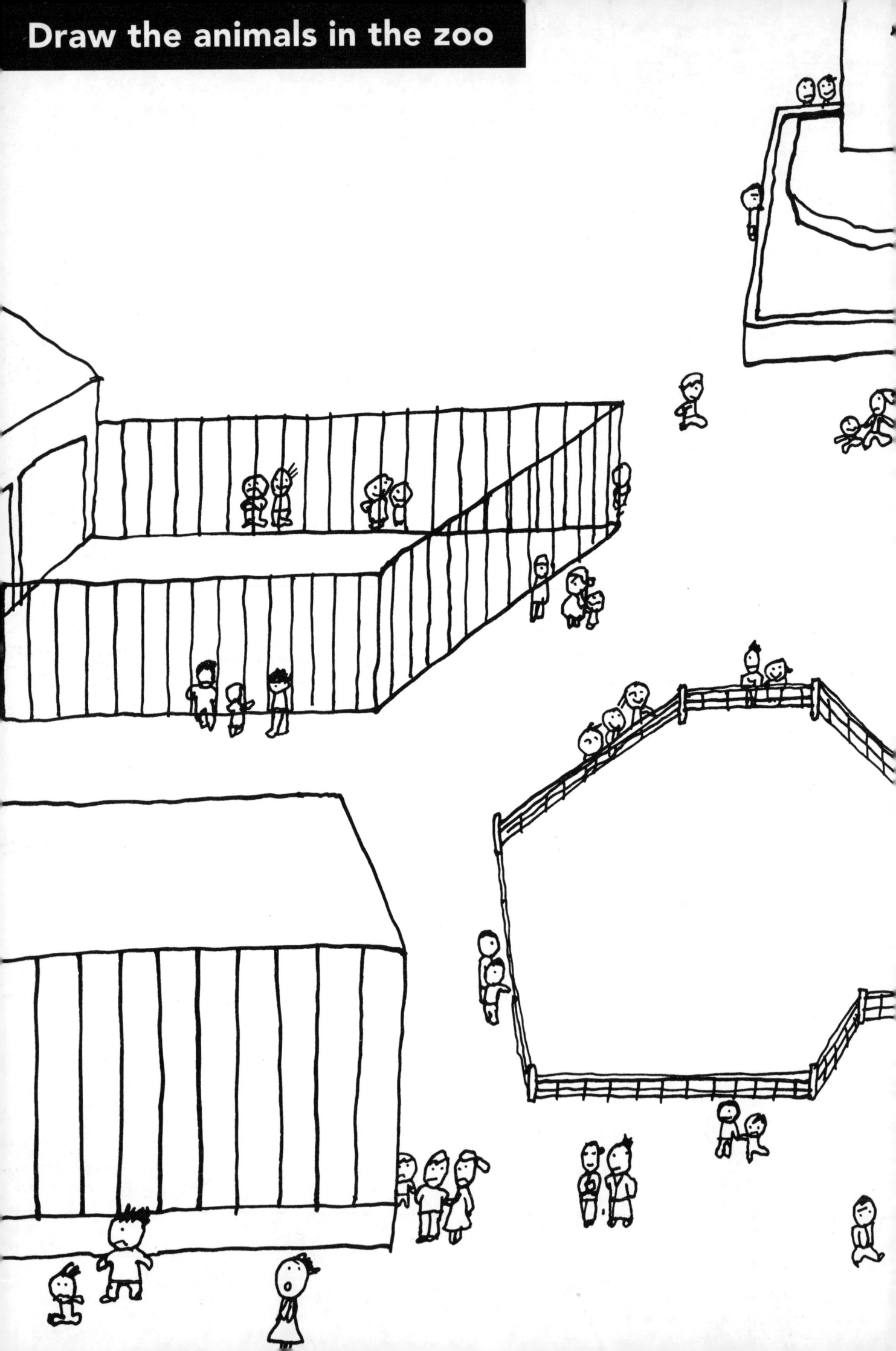

Make them howl or breathe fire

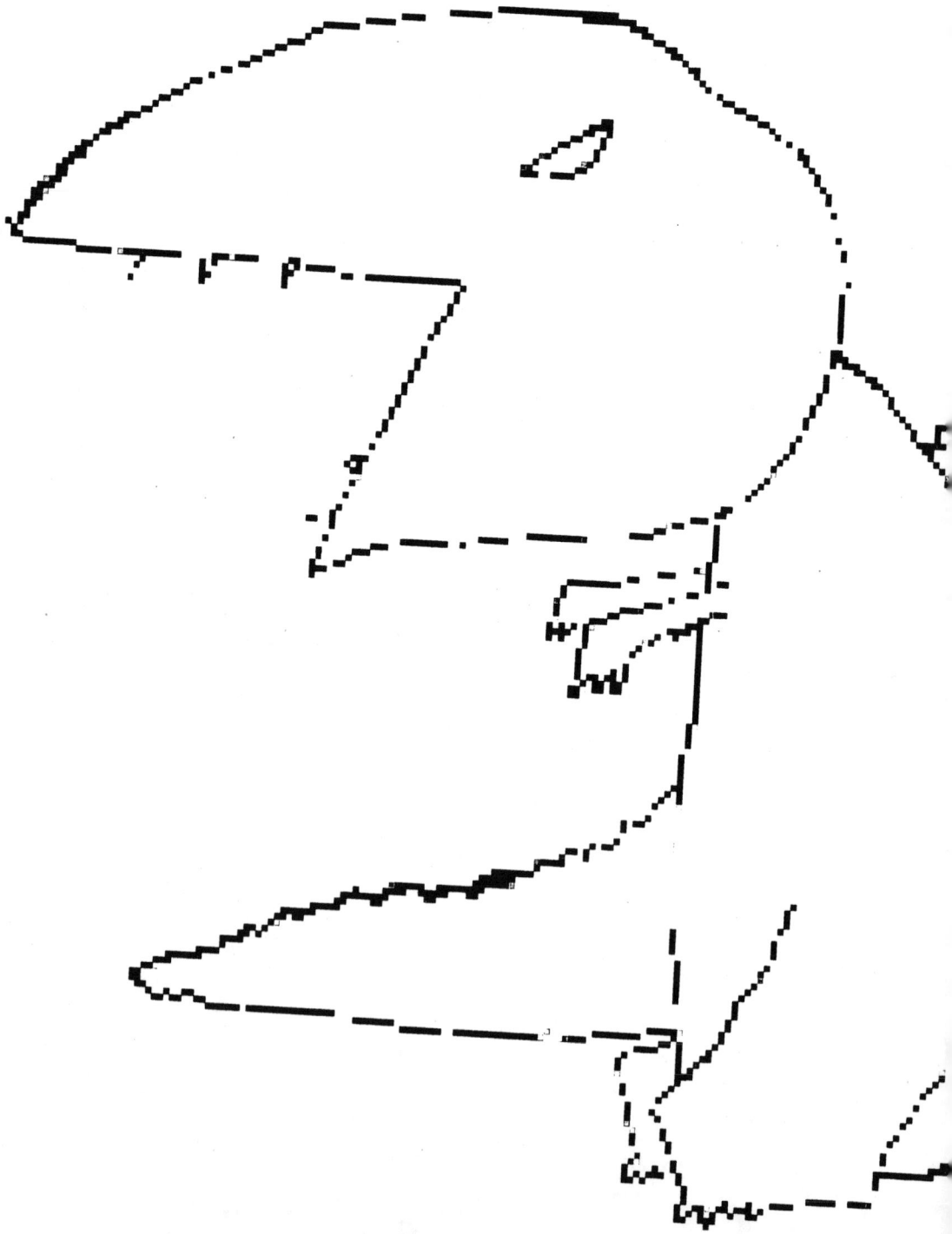

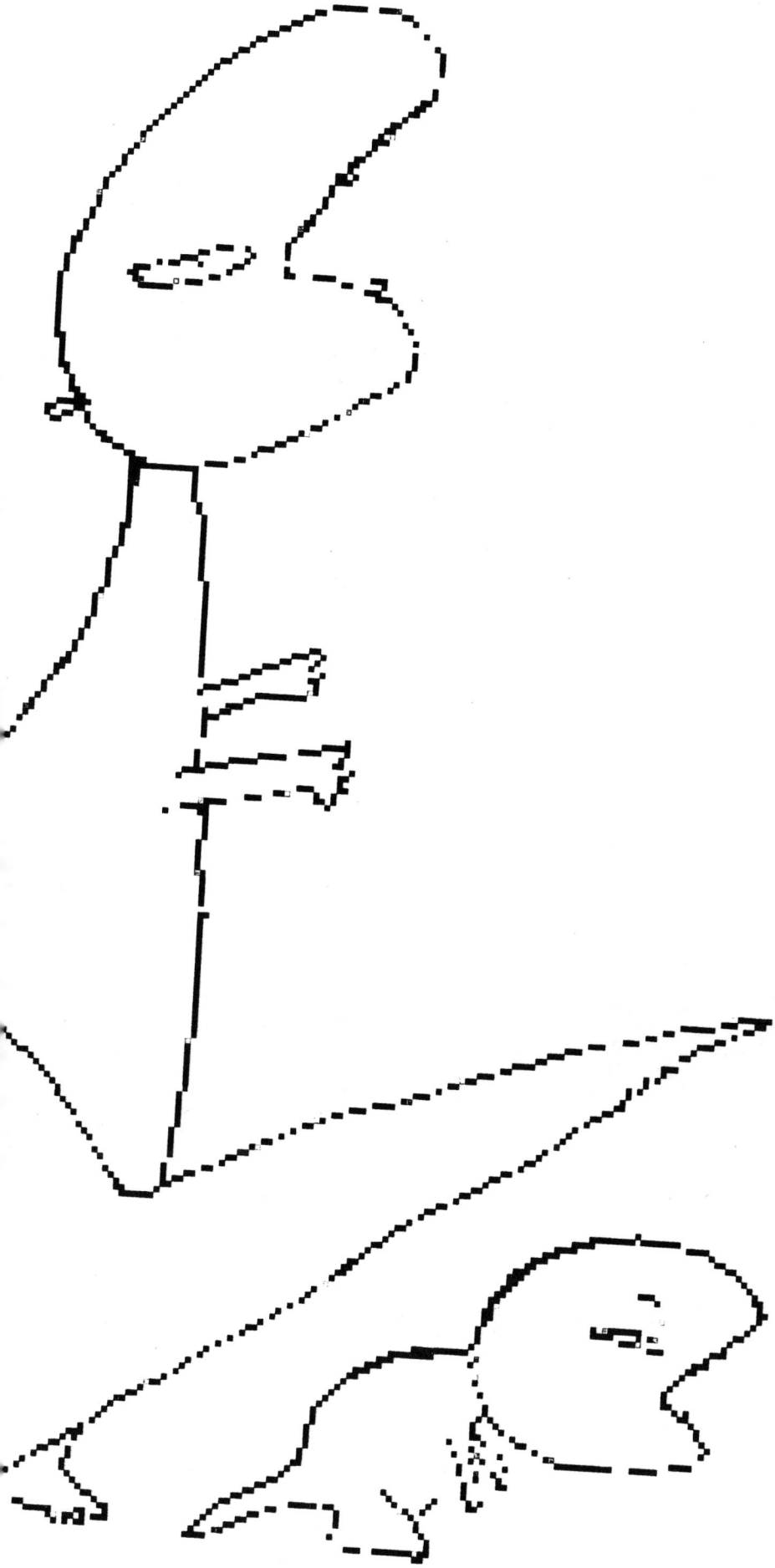

Draw a surfer

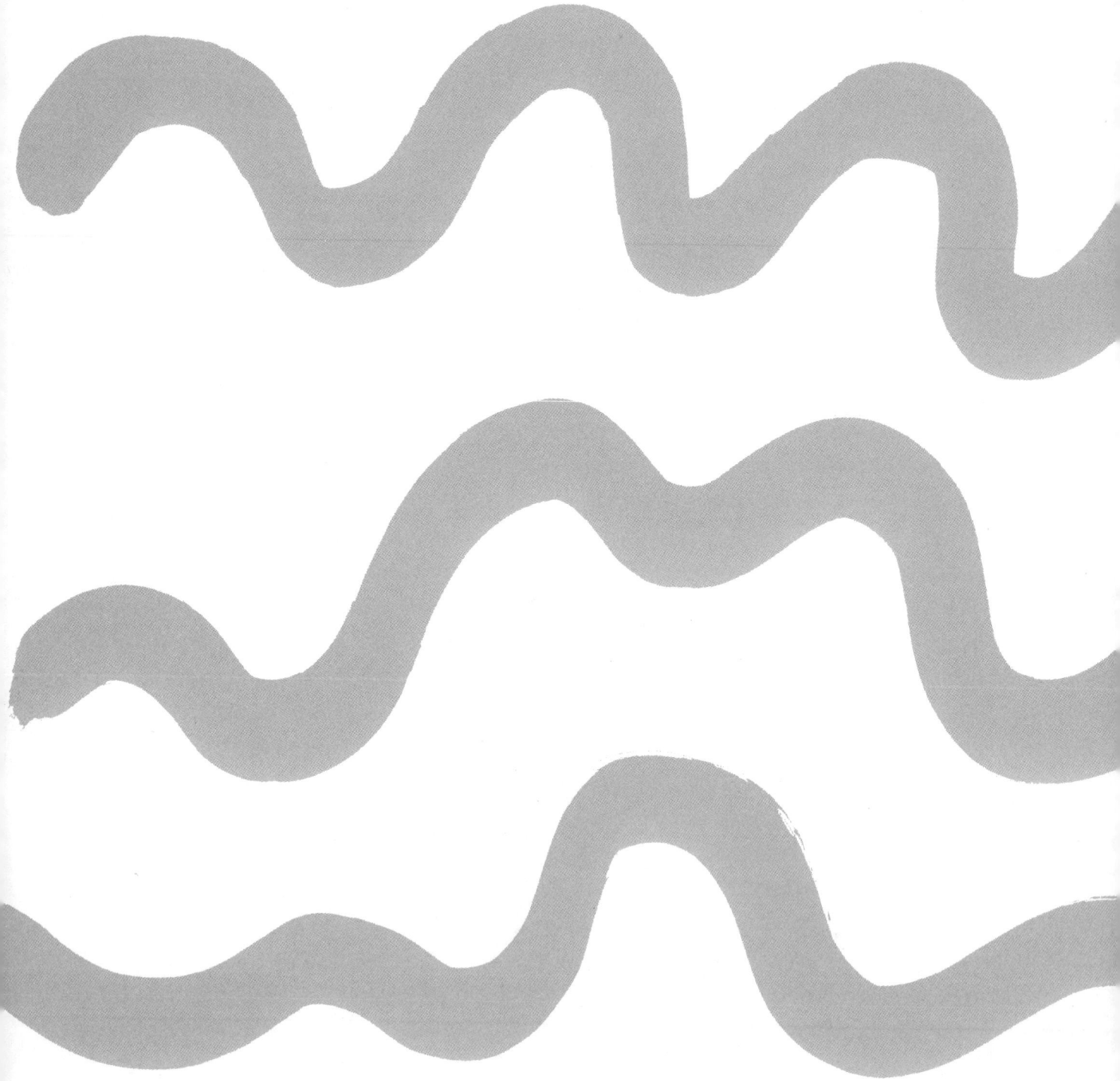

Back of the box

To make a box, cut along the dark lines, fold along the lighter lines, and glue down the tabs

You might want to color it first

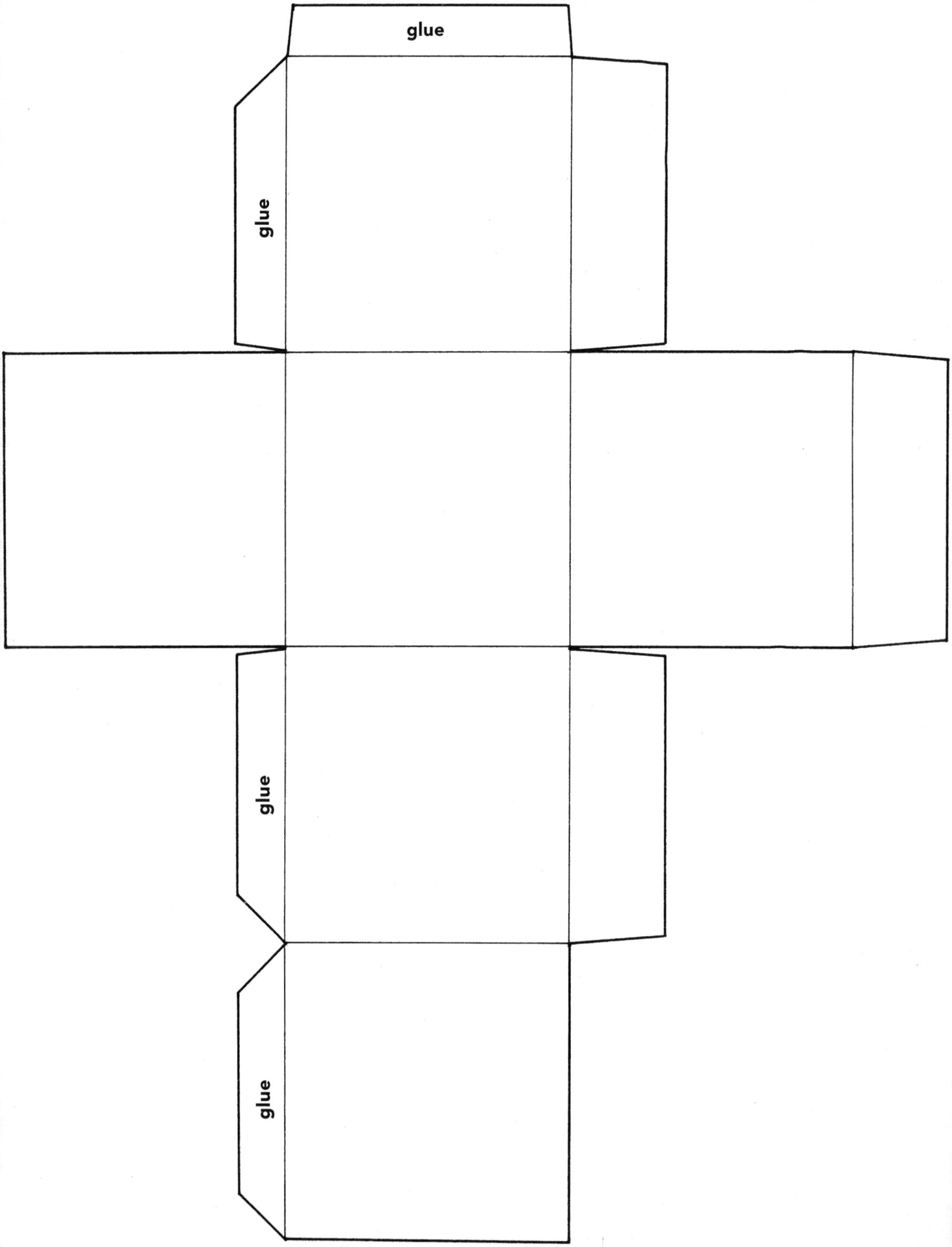

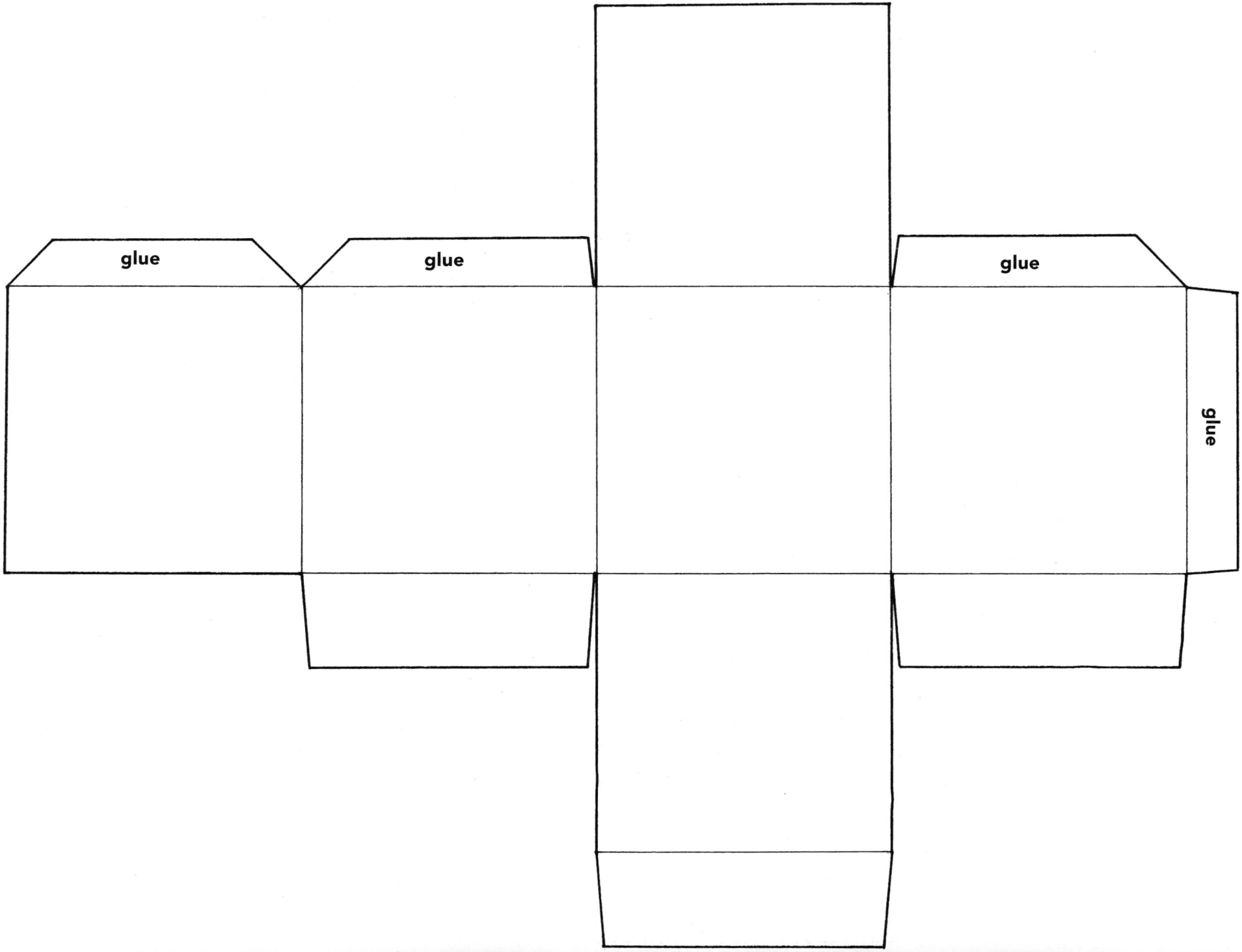
glue
glue
glue
glue

Back of the box

Color every other square

If it becomes too difficult, stop!

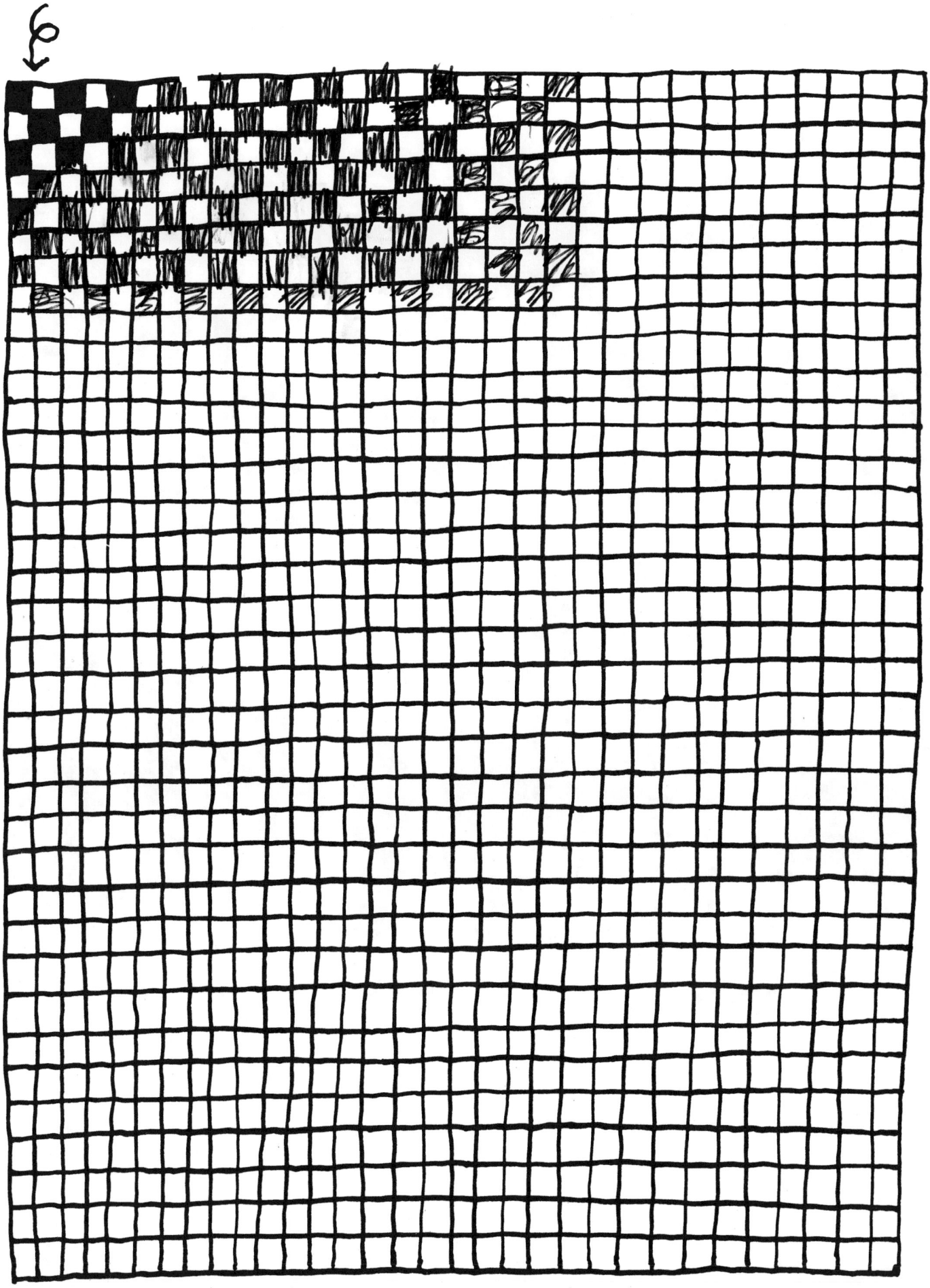

This is a tiger

Draw its stripes

This is a panther

Draw its black fur

This is a leopard

Draw its spots

Draw something beautiful

Draw something that begins with A

Draw something that begins with O

Draw lots of stars

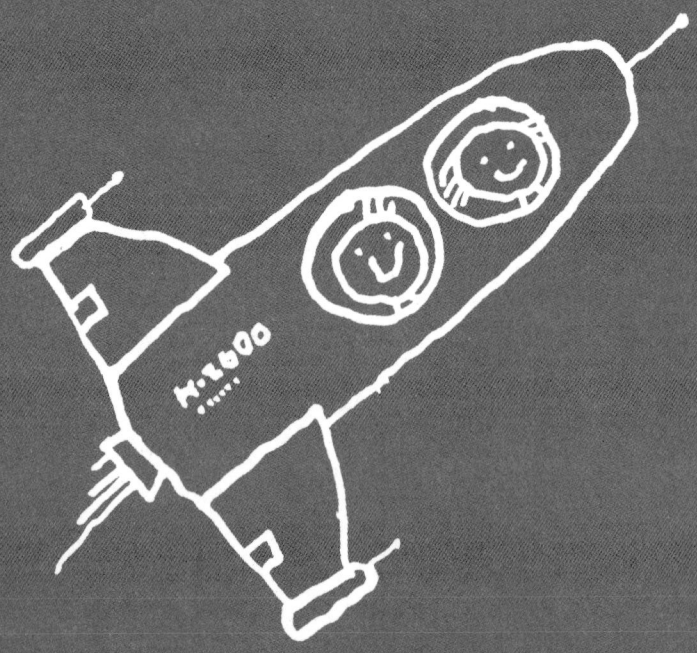

This is the jungle

Draw all the animals that are hiding

Put books on this bookcase

Back of the mask

These are masks

Color them and cut them out

Back of the mask

Back of the mask

These are masks, too

Back of the mask

Back of the mask

Here are more masks

The sun and a star

Star

Back of the mask

Back of the mask

And even more masks

Back of the mask

This is a maze

Try to get to the center

Scribble on this wall

Hurry up or you might get caught!

GAGE
WUZ
HERE

Draw a dead person

This is a mountain

Draw some mountain climbers

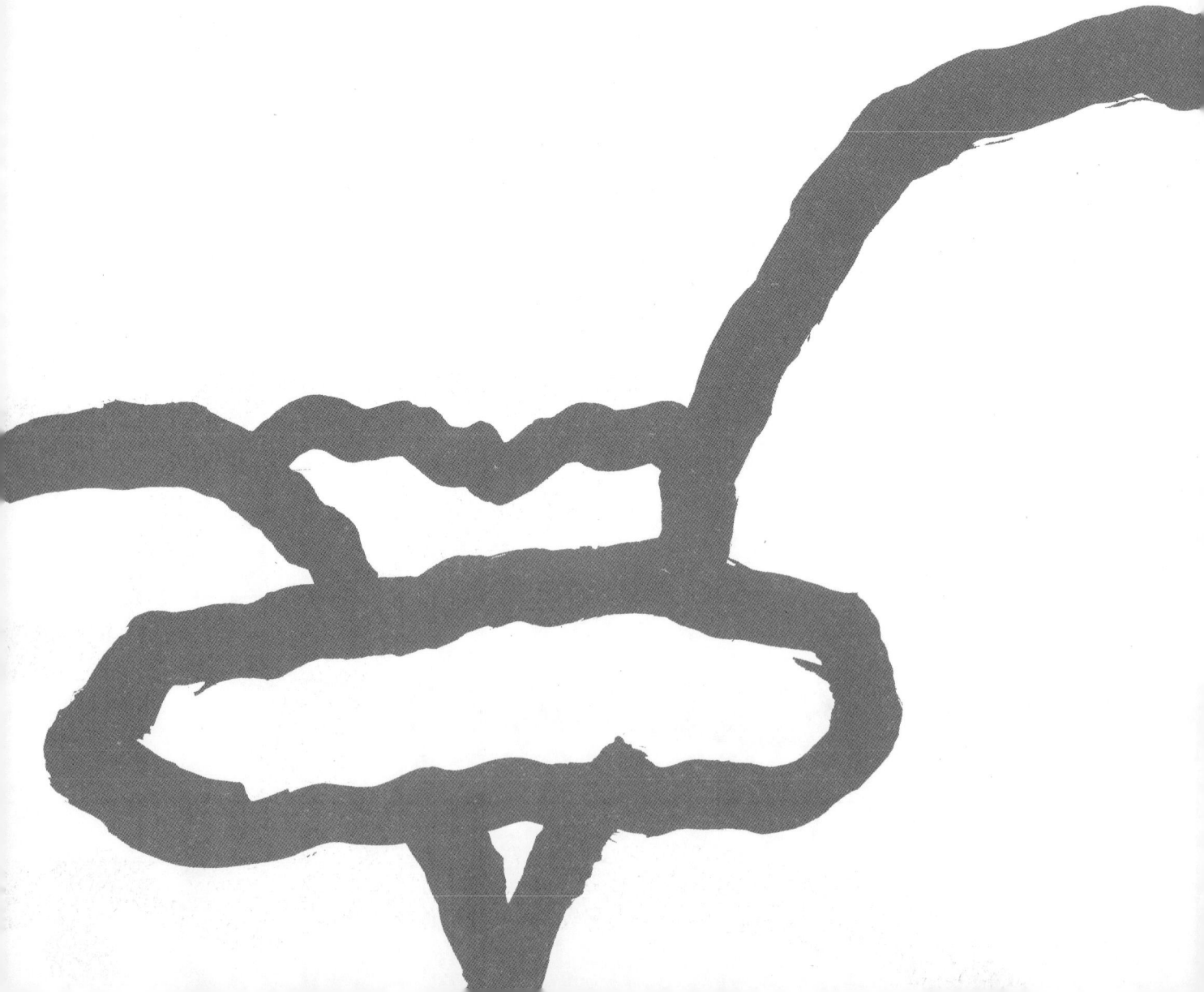

Load the truck

Correct them

because weather

To day, be cause the wether was not

nice

naice, my father and i went to the

moovies. After that, we brought some

post cards in a toi shoppe. We were

very pleased toy tomorrow weather

veri pleesed. Tommorrow, the wether

wont either

wount to be nice eithir.

Write what you did today

Without any mistakes, please!

What are they carrying?

Do you have to go to the bathroom, Billy?
ABC
POWER IS BEST.
1000000 lbs
1000000 lbs

This is a bowl of soup

Draw the ingredients

This is a bowl of broth

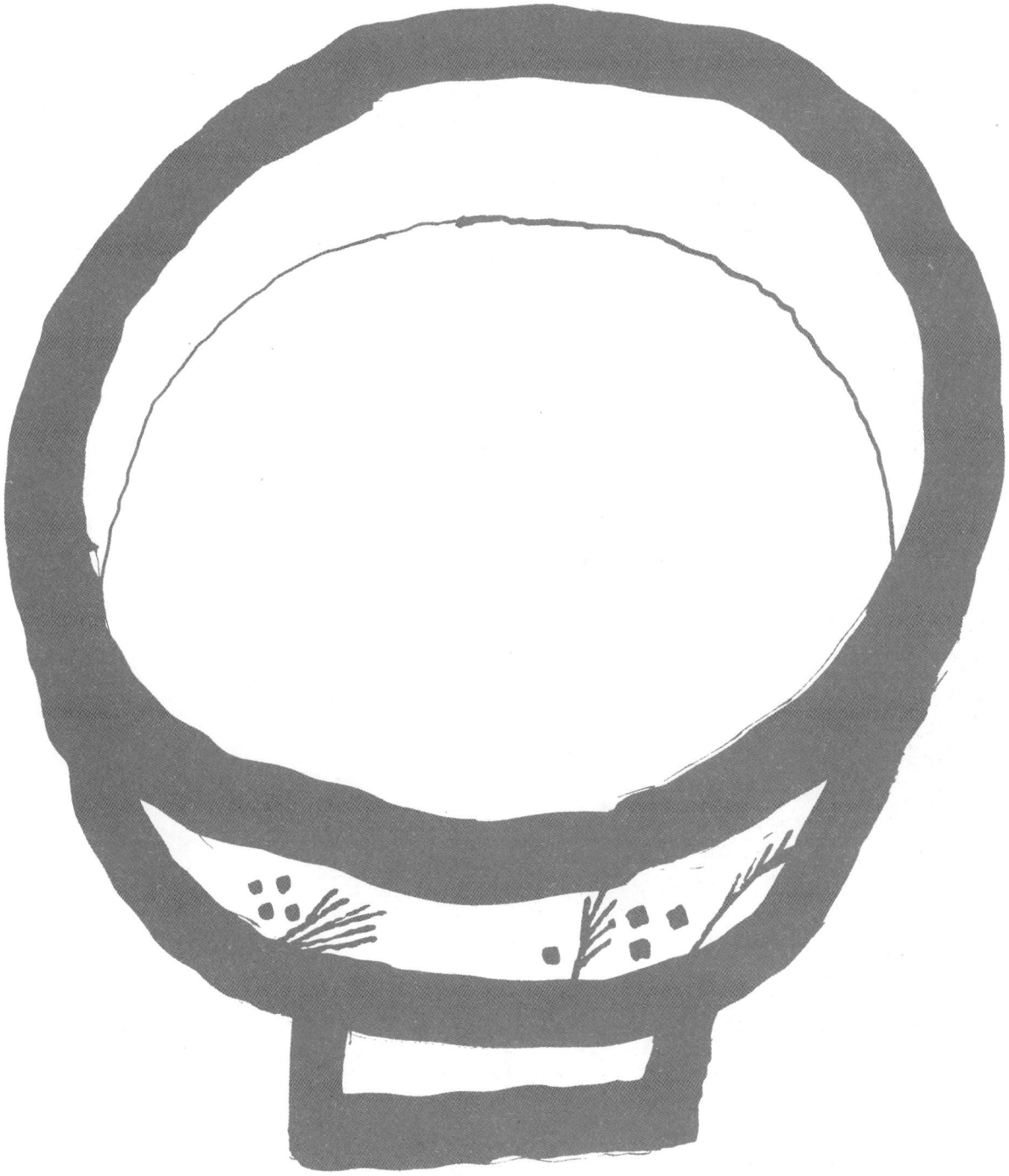

Draw the sounds coming out of the trumpet

Draw the sounds coming from the drum

Put some appointments on your calendar

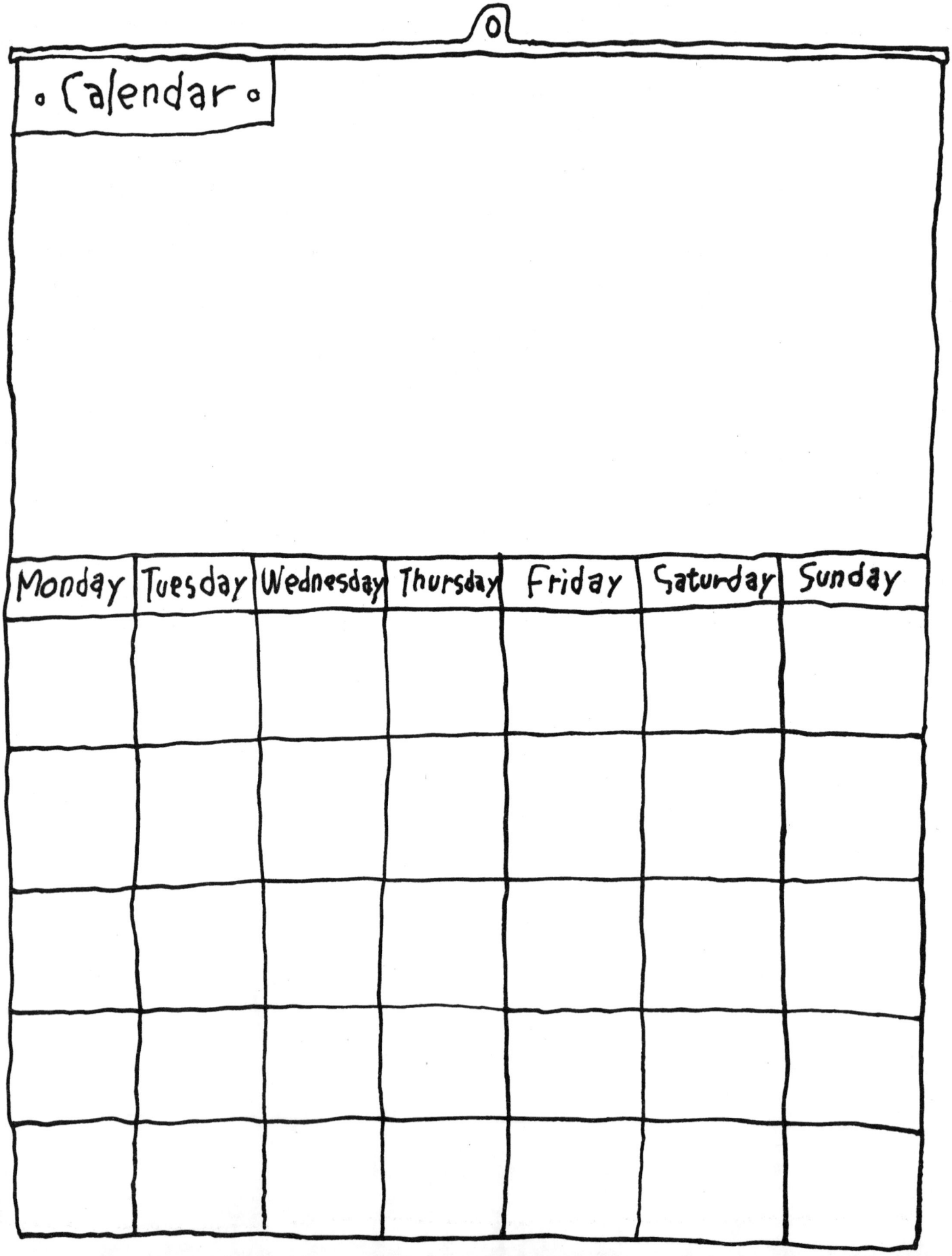

CALENDAR.
MON
TUE
WED
THU
SAT.
日 SUN.
月 MON.
火 TUE.
水 WED.
木 THU.
金 FRI.
土 SAT.

This is a forest

Draw the animals hiding among the trees

Draw some people inside the shape

Draw some people outside the shape

Fill this swimming pool with water

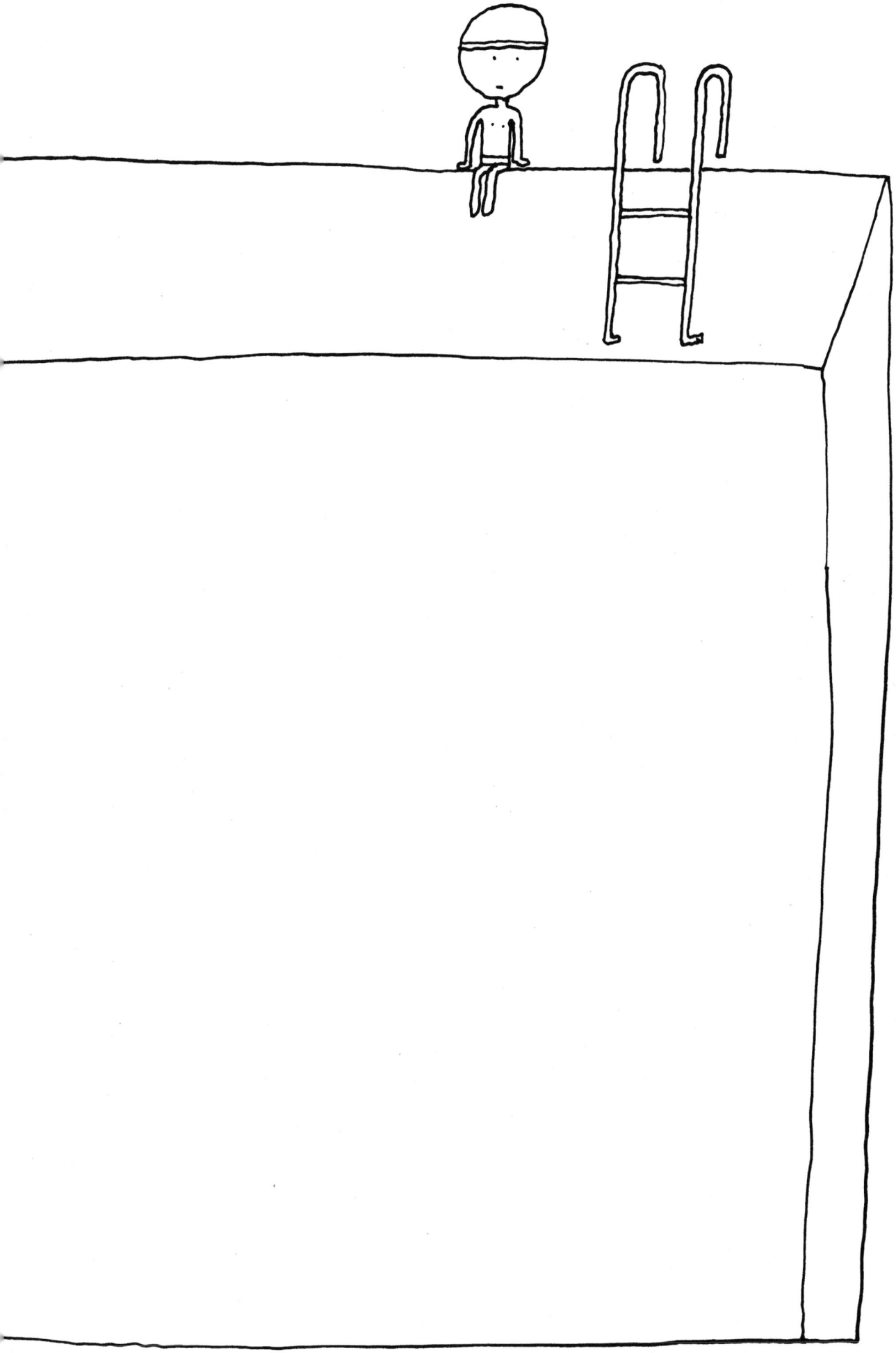

Fill this room with furniture

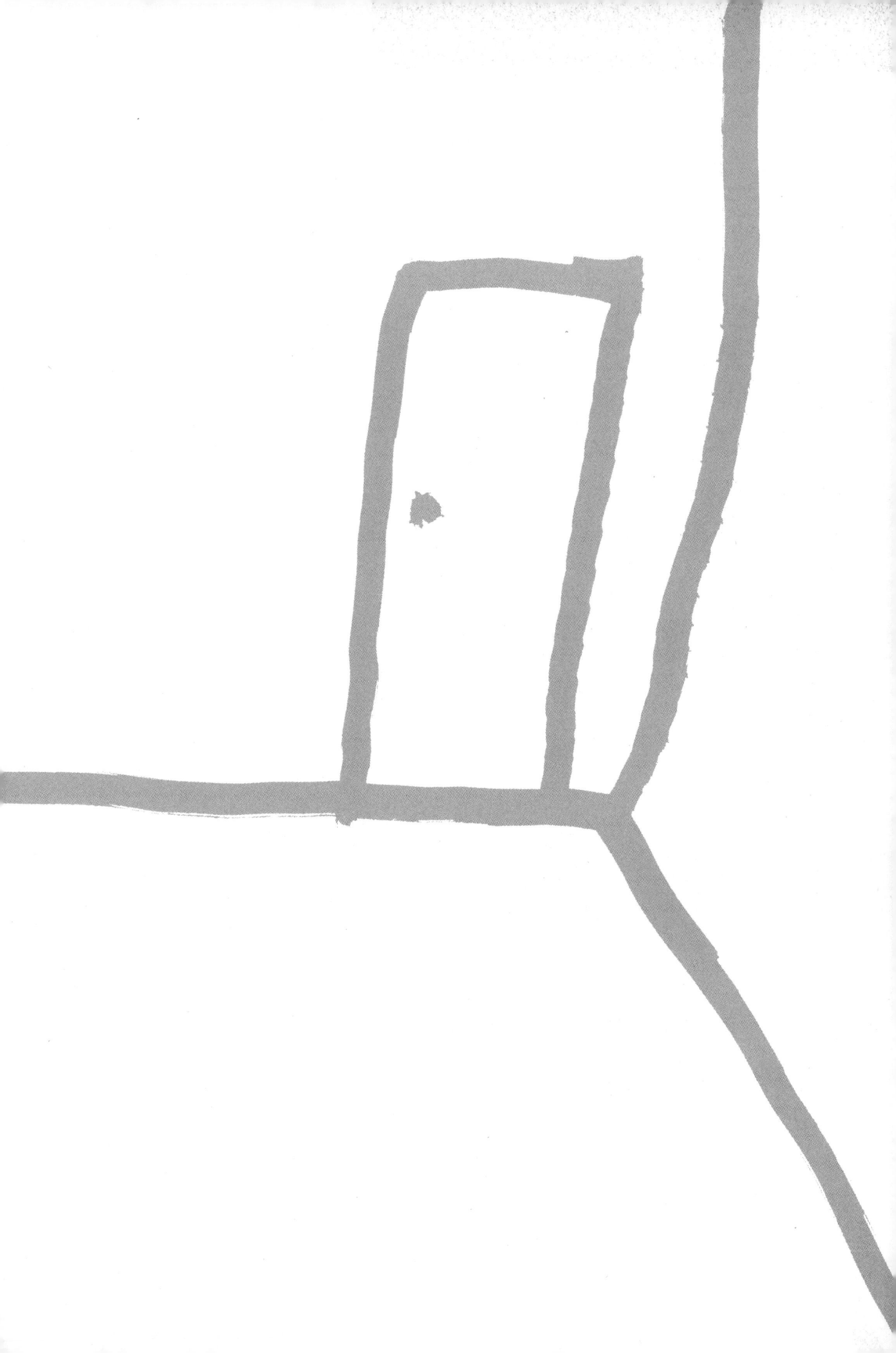

Draw on these empty canvasses

Imagine what these people would paint

Draw fireworks

This is a park

Draw people walking around

This rag and these shoes are very dirty

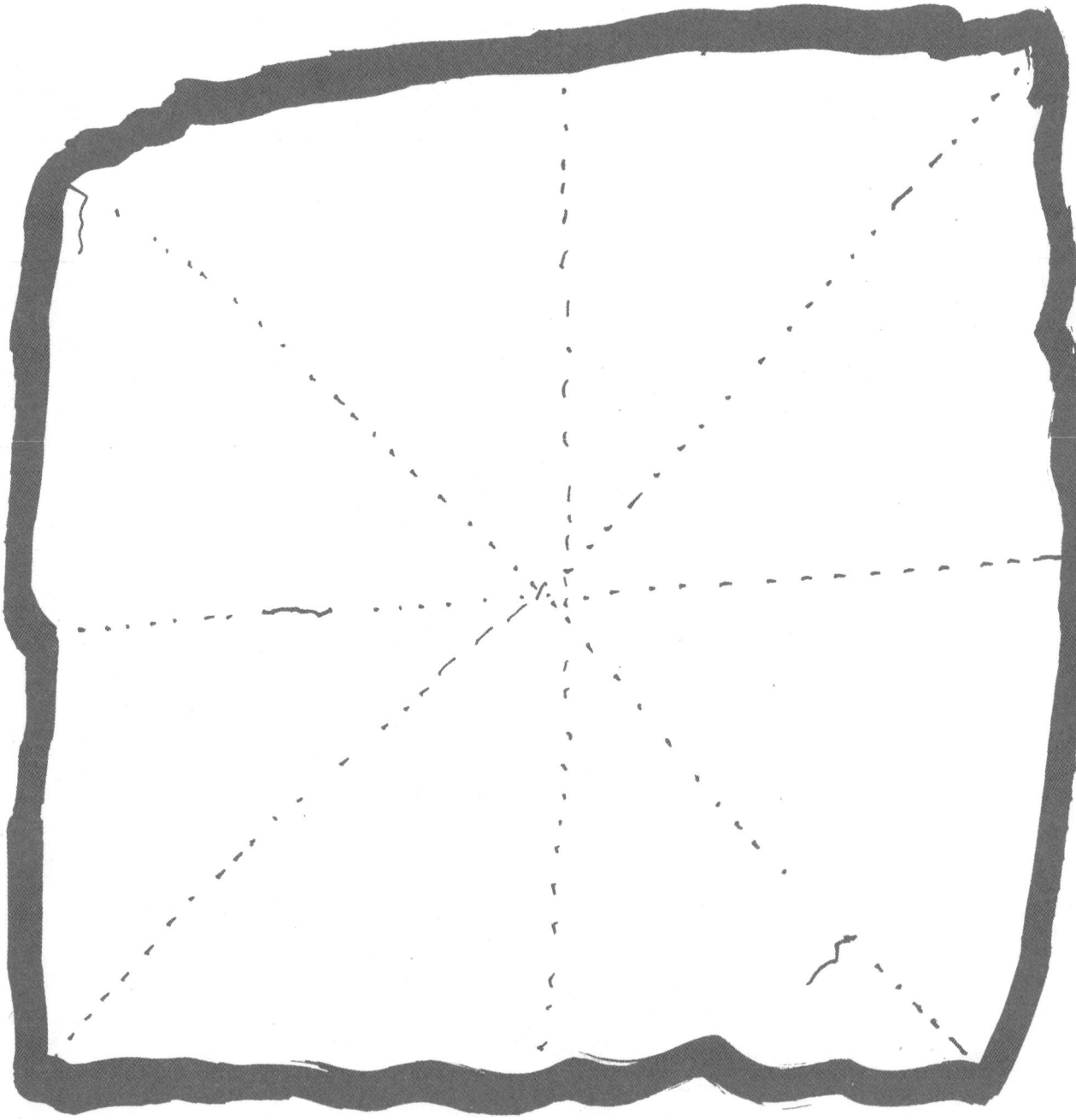

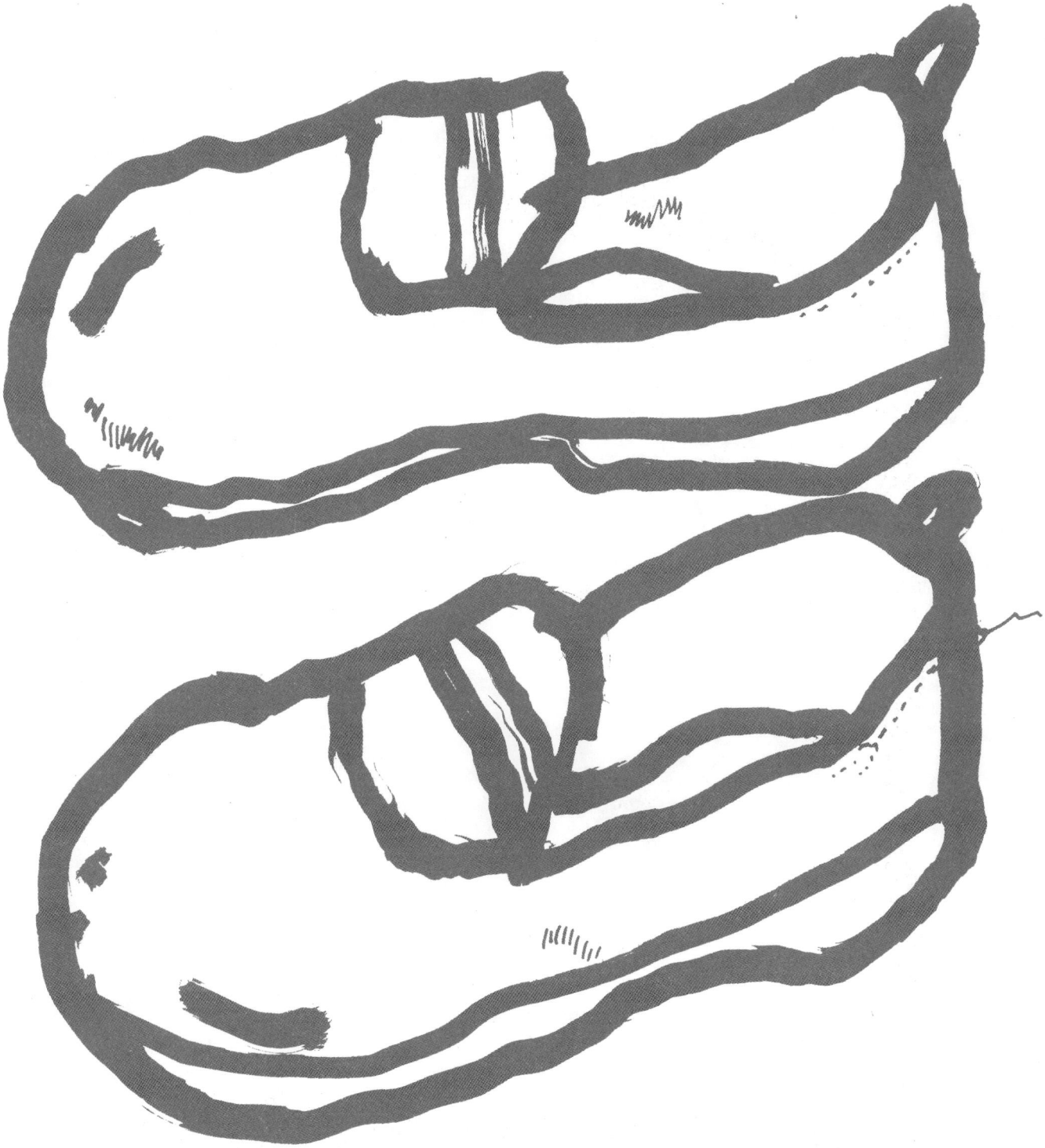

Draw lots of gravy, too

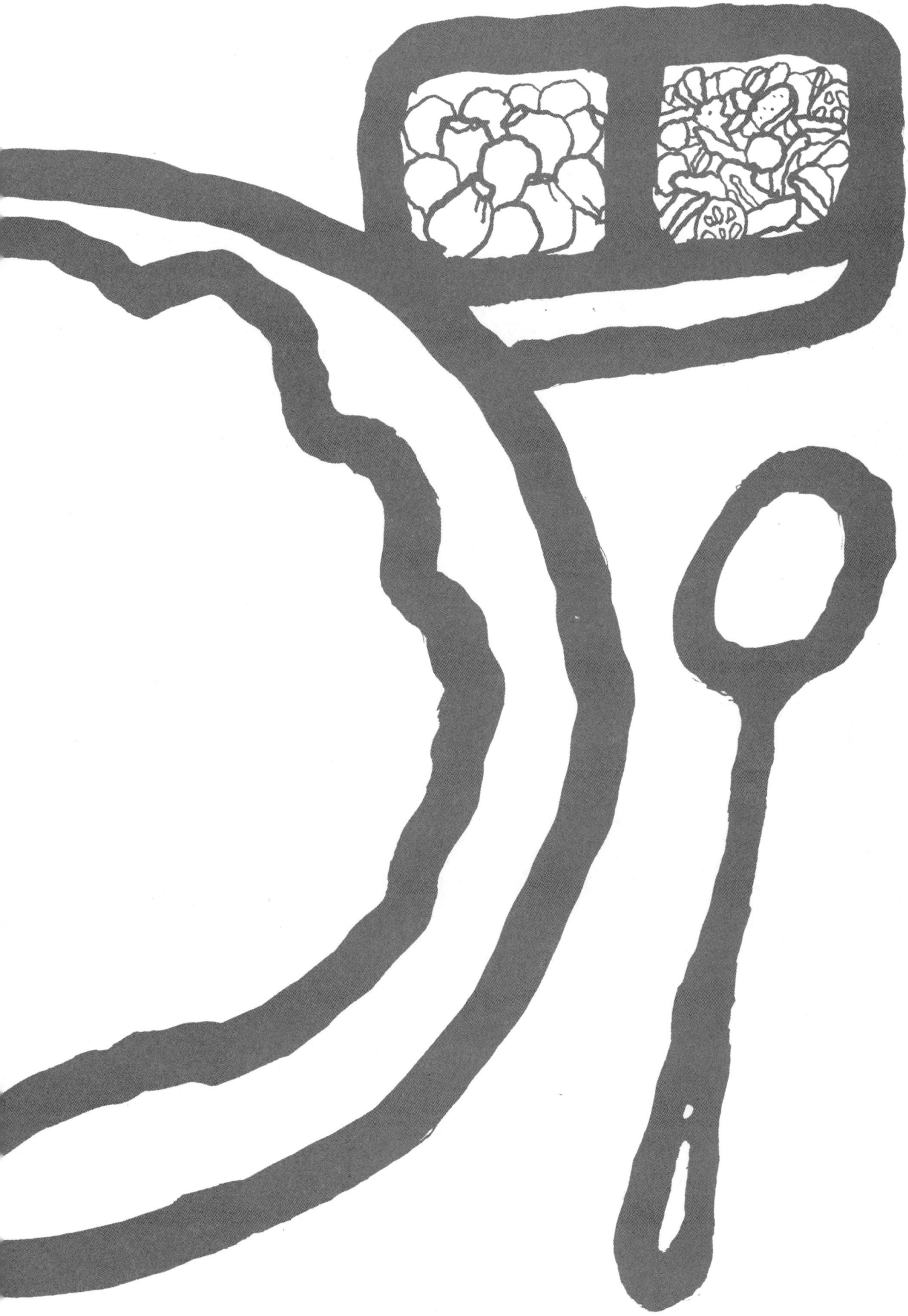

Wham! It's a fly ball!

Draw the person who's going to catch the ball

These are cherry trees in bloom

Draw the people who have come to admire them

What's on the ground here?

Make these pastries look delicious

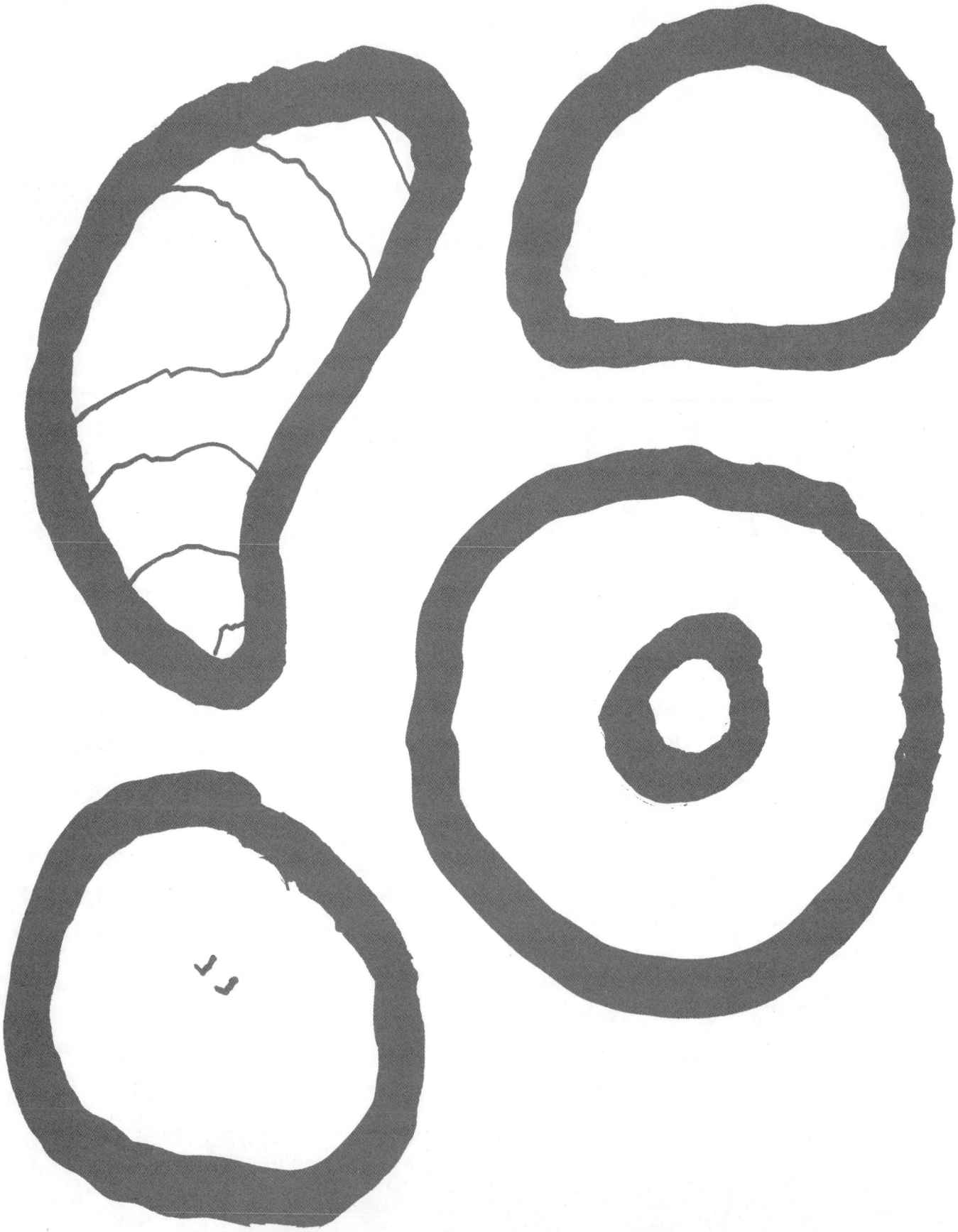

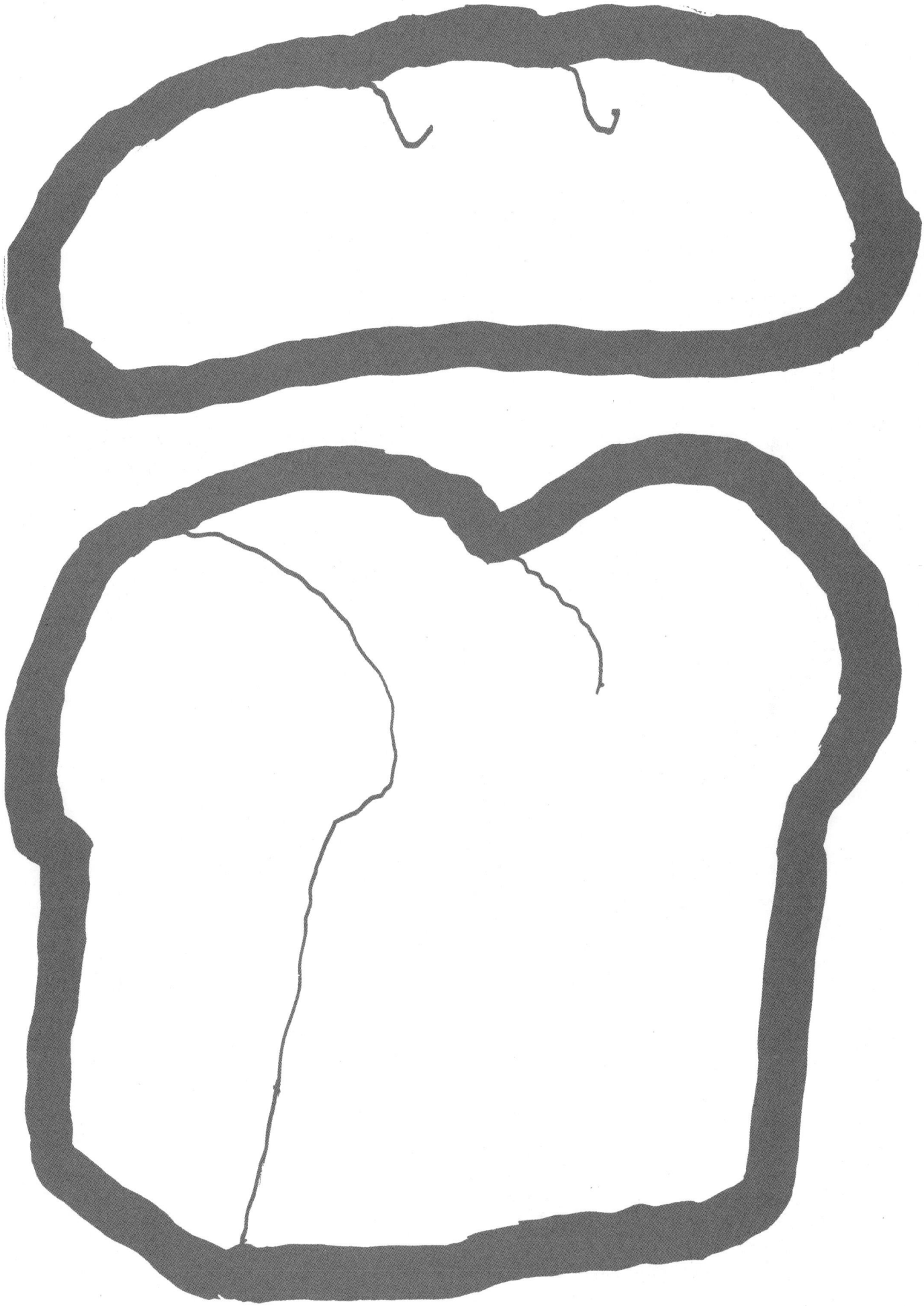

These are lockers

Number them in the right order

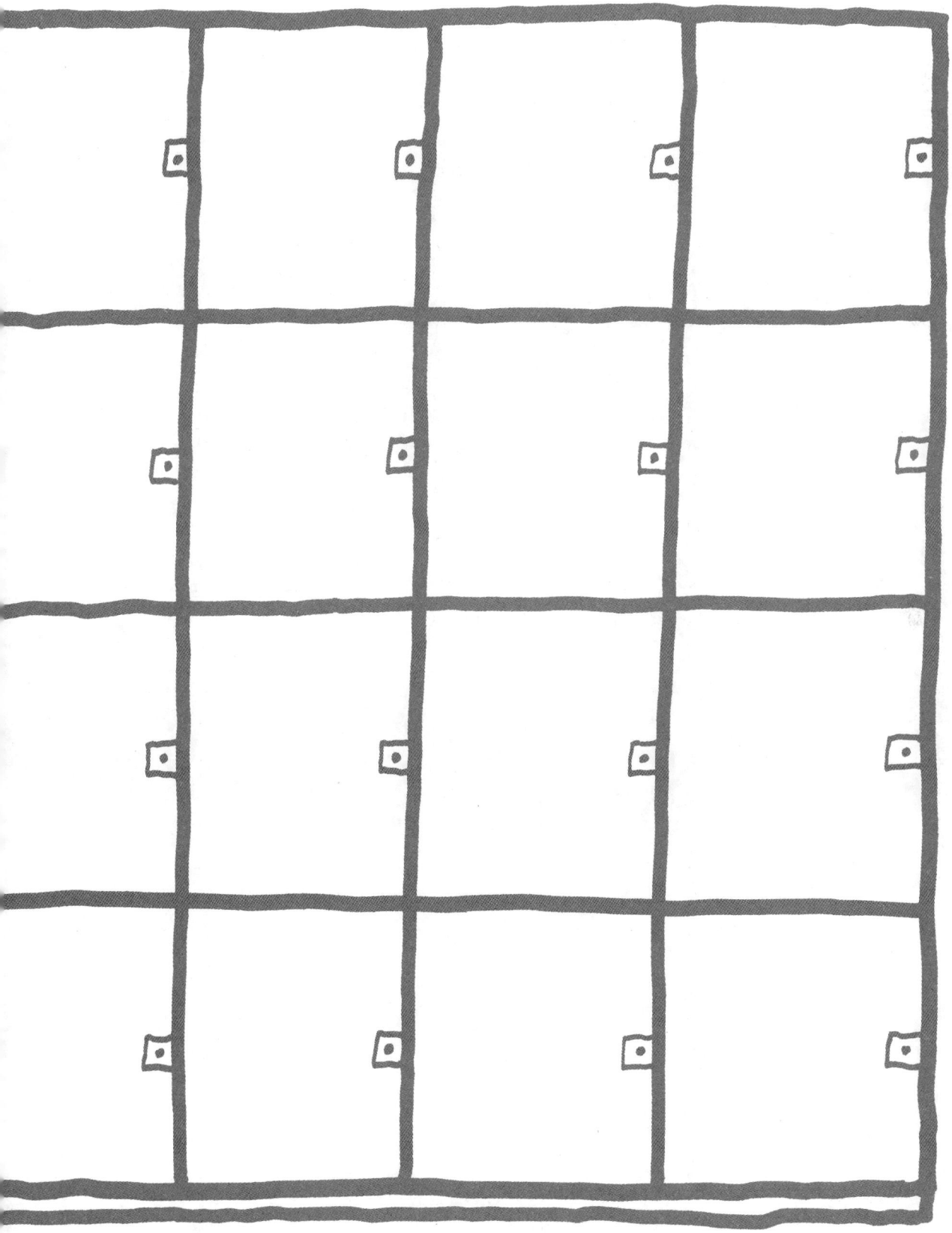

Draw a skeleton

Secret

Draw something secret

Then cut it out and hide it

cut

This is a postcard

Draw and write something that happened to you and cut it out

cut

cut

Back of the postcard

Back of the envelope

Write a letter and put it in the envelope

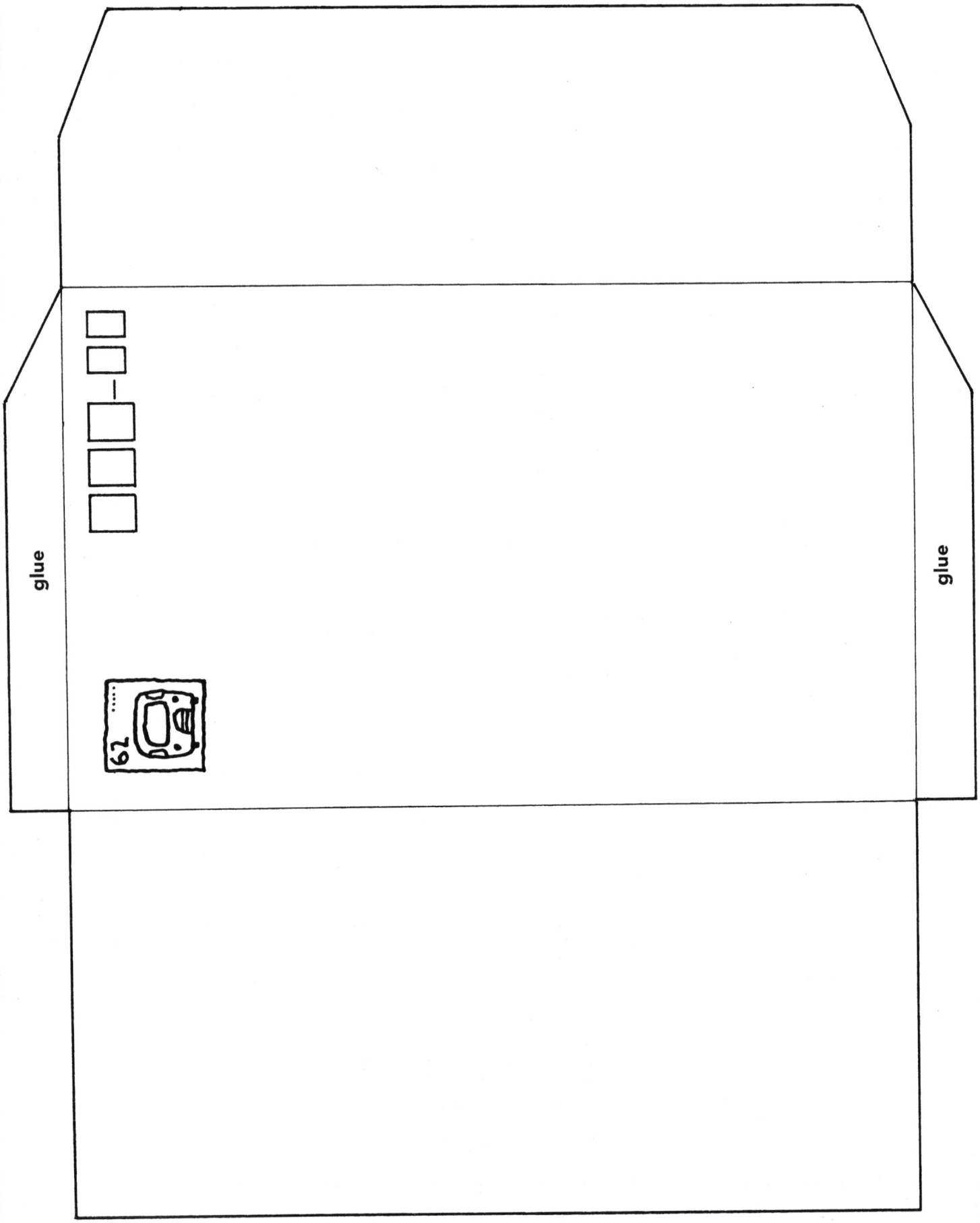

Back of the stationery

Back of the envelope

Write another letter

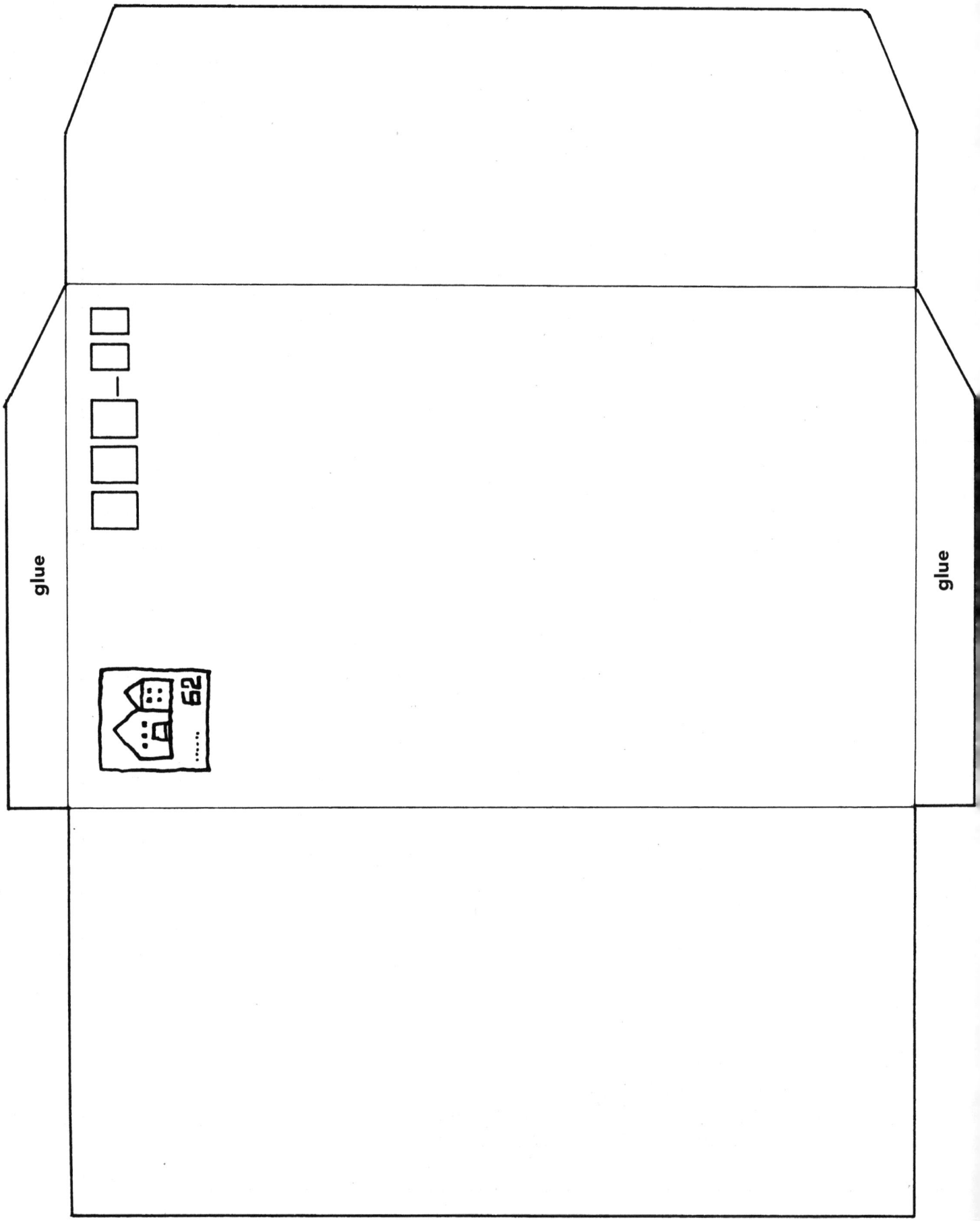

Back of the stationery

Back of the envelope

And another letter

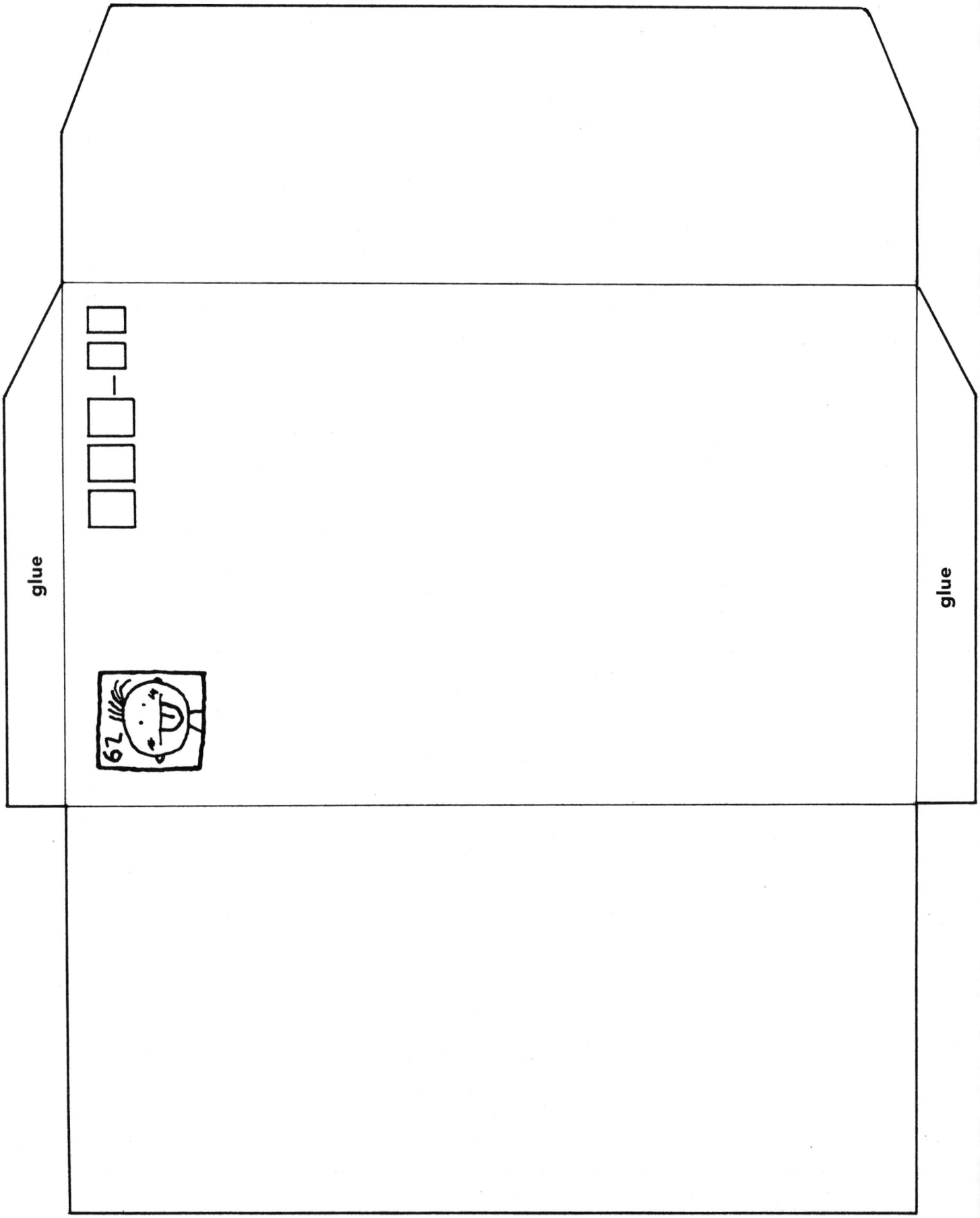

Back of the stationery

Draw a self-portrait

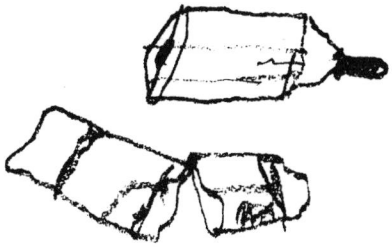

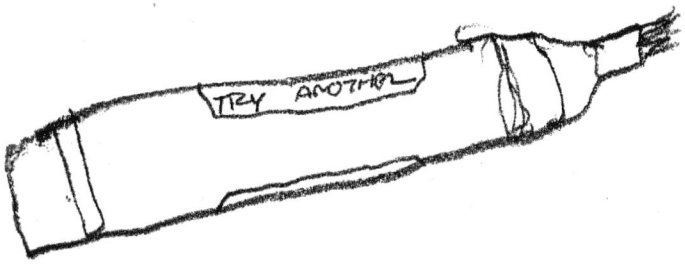

YOUR
CARD.